Music, Books and Theatre in Eighteenth-Century Exton

This book establishes the cultural background to the productions of Milton's *Comus* that were staged in the 1740s by Baptist Noel, 4th Earl of Gainsborough, at Exton Hall, his country seat in the East Midlands of England.

The author reveals that Handel's visit in 1745 occurred in a richer and fuller context of cultural interests among the Noel family. Most of the music at Exton was selected from existing works by Handel, but the four movements of the finale were new, written by the composer specifically for the occasion. The study is based on receipted bills and other documents in an archival collection of Noel family papers that provide evidence of the Earl's purchase of books and music and of the musical and theatrical activities undertaken on his Exton estate. The author discusses the Earl's interests in music, books and theatre, indicating a belief in performance as a valuable and enjoyable experience and as a vehicle for the education of the young. In addition to creating a context for *Comus*, this book sheds light on cultural life in a mid-eighteenth-century English country house and how the Earl's productions made a significant contribution to the cultural life of the East Midlands.

The book will be of great value to cultural musicologists, historians and Handelians, as the documentation sheds a huge amount of light on a variety of cultural practices in eighteenth-century England.

Colin Timms is Emeritus Professor of Music at the University of Birmingham, UK. He has published mainly on Steffani, Stradella and Handel, and edited music by all three composers. His edition of *Comus* (music by Handel and Arne) appeared in 2016, his study of its verbal and musical text in 2022.

Royal Musical Association Monographs
Series Editor: Catherine A. Bradley

This series was originally supported by funds made available to the Royal Musical Association from the estate of Thurston Dart, former King Edward Professor of Music at the University of London. The editorial board is the Publications Committee of the Association.

No. 35: *Felice Giardini and Professional Music Culture in mid-eighteenth-century London*
Cheryll Duncan

No. 36: *Disinformation in Mass Media: Gluck, Piccinni and the Journal de Paris*
Beverly Jerold

No. 37: *Music Theory in Late Medieval Avignon: Music Theory in Late Medieval Avignon*
Karen M. Cook

No. 38: *Gregorio Ballabene's Forty-eight-part Mass for Twelve Choirs (1772)*
Florian Bassani

No. 39: *Authorship and Identity in Late Thirteenth-Century Motets*
Catherine A. Bradley

No. 40: *The Malmariée in the Thirteenth-Century Motet*
Dolores Pesce

No. 41: *Music, Books and Theatre in Eighteenth-Century Exton: A Context for Handel's 'Comus'*
Colin Timms

No. 42: *Return to Riemann: Tonal Function and Chromatic Music*
J. P. E. Harper-Scott and Oliver Chandler

For more information about this series, please visit: www.routledge.com/music/series/RMA

Music, Books and Theatre in Eighteenth-Century Exton
A Context for Handel's 'Comus'

Colin Timms

LONDON AND NEW YORK

First published 2024
by Routledge
4 Park Square, Milton Park, Abingdon, Oxon OX14 4RN

and by Routledge
605 Third Avenue, New York, NY 10158

Routledge is an imprint of the Taylor & Francis Group, an informa business

© 2024 Colin Timms

The right of Colin Timms to be identified as author of this work has been asserted in accordance with sections 77 and 78 of the Copyright, Designs and Patents Act 1988.

All rights reserved. No part of this book may be reprinted or reproduced or utilised in any form or by any electronic, mechanical, or other means, now known or hereafter invented, including photocopying and recording, or in any information storage or retrieval system, without permission in writing from the publishers.

Trademark notice: Product or corporate names may be trademarks or registered trademarks, and are used only for identification and explanation without intent to infringe.

British Library Cataloguing-in-Publication Data
A catalogue record for this book is available from the British Library

Library of Congress Cataloging-in-Publication Data
Names: Timms, Colin, author.
Title: Music, books and theatre in eighteenth-century Exton: a context for Handel's 'Comus'/Colin Timms.
Description: [1.] | Abingdon, Oxon; New York: Routledge, 2024. | Series: Royal Musical Association monographs | Includes bibliographical references and index.
Identifiers: LCCN 2023047278 (print) | LCCN 2023047279 (ebook) | ISBN 9781032627816 (hardback) | ISBN 9781032627854 (paperback) | ISBN 9781032627915 (ebook)
Subjects: LCSH: Masques with music–18th century–History and criticism. | Music patronage–England–Rutland–History–18th century. | Gainsborough, Baptist Noel, Earl of, 1708-1751. | Handel, George Frideric, 1685-1759. There in blissful shades and bow'rs. | Milton, John, 1608-1674. Comus. | Exton Hall (Rutland, England)
Classification: LCC ML1731.7.R87 T45 2024 (print) | LCC ML1731.7.R87 (ebook) | DDC 782.10942/09032–dc23/eng/20231017
LC record available at https://lccn.loc.gov/2023047278
LC ebook record available at https://lccn.loc.gov/2023047279

ISBN: 9781032627816 (hbk)
ISBN: 9781032627854 (pbk)
ISBN: 9781032627915 (ebk)

DOI: 10.4324/9781032627915

Typeset in Times New Roman
by Deanta Global Publishing Services, Chennai, India

Contents

List of Illustrations   *vii*
List of Music Examples   *viii*
Acknowledgements   *ix*

Introduction   1
    Notes   3

1   The 4th Earl of Gainsborough   4
    Subscriptions to Books and Music   12
    Notes   21

2   Evidence from the Archives   26
    Books   27
    Music   32
       Instruments   33
       Purchase of Music   34
       Binding   37
       Paper and Copying   38
       Performance   39
    Theatre   41
       Stages and Scenery   41
       Repertory   44
       Productions   45
    Notes   50

3   Gainsborough's Legacy   54
    Notes   59

Appendix I: Subscriptions and Dedications   61
    Baptist Noel, 4th Earl of Gainsborough   61
        Books   61
        Music   62
    Dorothy Noel (née Manners), Dowager Countess of
        Gainsborough   63
    Elizabeth Noel (née Chapman), Countess of
        Gainsborough   63
    Notes   64

Appendix II: Documents on Music, Books and Theatre   65
    Documents and Commentaries   65
    Index to the Documents   99
        Books   99
            Positive Identifications (short titles)   100
            Uncertain Identifications   107
            Unidentified Items   109
        Music   109
            Compositions (short titles)   109
            Instruments (including strings, bows, etc.)   110
        Plays   110
        Theatre   111

Bibliography   112
Index   118

Illustrations

1.1 Baptist Noel, 4th Earl of Gainsborough. Portrait by
 J. Henesy, signed and dated 1737   7
1.2 Exton Park. Engraving by John Harris (*c.* 1739) after a
 painting by Thomas Badeslade   8
1.3 Exton Park. Engraving by James Mason (*c.* 1749) after a
 painting by Thomas Smith   9
1.4 Michael Christian Festing, *Twelve Sonatas in Three Parts*
 [...] *Opera secunda* (London: Printed by William Smith
 [...] and Sold only by the Author, 1731). Part of the list of
 subscribers   14
1.5 Richard Browne, *Medicina Musica: or, A Mechanical Essay
 on the Effects of Singing, Musick, and Dancing, on Human
 Bodies* [...] (London: John Cooke, 1729). Title page   16

Music Examples

1.1 F. Marchant, 'As Persians stretch their votive arms'.
    Transcription from a printed song sheet (*c.* 1730), bars 1–16   19
1.2 Anon., 'The Persians stretch their votive arms'.
    Transcription from British Library, Add. MS 31806, f. 20,
    bars 1–7   20
2.1 ['Mr Gouge'], 'Fond Echo, forbear thy light strain', bars
    1–32. Transcription from an anonymous song sheet entitled
    *The Forsaken Maid. A New Song in the Tragedy Call'd
    Double Falsehood by Shakespear* [*c.* 1728]   48

Acknowledgements

This study is an attempt to establish the background to the productions of Milton's 'Comus' at Exton in 1745, for which Handel composed the finale, and in 1748. My interest in this subject rests on foundations laid by others, sadly no longer with us. That such performances had taken place at the country seat of the 4th Earl of Gainsborough and that Handel had contributed to them was completely unknown before 1959, when Betty Matthews published two contemporary letters that mention them. Ten years later Anthony Hicks discovered the composer's finale and subsequently invited me to help prepare an edition of the setting, then unknown. Hicks later found a contemporary list of pre-existing movements by Handel that had been incorporated into the masque, which he discussed at a conference in 2001, nine years before he died. Having since published an edition of the complete work and written a separate study of its verbal and musical text, I decided to investigate the context in which the seemingly isolated performances of the 1740s had been conceived and presented. I was keen to find out, in particular, how broad and deep the musical and theatrical interests of the earl and his family were, and how, if at all, these interests found expression in their life at Exton Hall.

The search for information soon led to the Record Office for Leicestershire, Leicester and Rutland, where a substantial collection of family documents had been placed on deposit in 1987 and augmented in 1990 and 1991; the hunt for material relating to music and theatre also revealed that Gainsborough had purchased books on a wide range of subjects. Hence the title and focus of this study. An interim report on my findings was presented as a paper to the Handel Institute conference on 'Handel and his Music for Patrons' at The Foundling Museum, London, in November 2018, and an article based on one of the documents – a letter from Roubiliac about Gainsborough's purchase of a bust of Handel – was published in the *Händel-Jahrbuch* for 2021. Those short accounts are exceeded in scope by the present study which, by investigating the interests of a mid-eighteenth-century English peer who embraced, explored, practised and encouraged the arts, provides a fuller background to the performances of *Comus* at Exton and sheds light on the cultural concerns and aspirations of the society to which he belonged.

x *Acknowledgements*

During the course of this research I have been assisted by a considerable number of people. I am particularly indebted to the staff of the Record Office for Leicestershire, Leicester and Rutland for their assistance during my visits to the archive in 2018, 2021 and 2022, and to Michael Talbot for reading and making constructive comments on an earlier version of this study. Adam Busiakiewicz supplied information on a number of Noel family portraits in a Sotheby's sale of April 2023, to which he drew my attention; Paul Spencer-Longhurst and Robert Wenley helped me investigate painters and sculptors; Carole Taylor shared her findings on the cultural and musical interests of the 3rd Duke of Rutland, and Vicki Perry found an important reference in his archives at Belvoir Castle. Cheryll Duncan gave advice on stringed instruments in eighteenth-century London; Simon D. I. Fleming and Martin Perkins supplied information on subscribers to printed music; Matthew Gardner and Harry Diack Johnstone set me straight on the Society of the Temple of Apollo, and Carrie Churnside responded to a last-minute request for assistance.

I am also very grateful to the members of staff who, even during the coronavirus pandemic, provided information on, and scans of, items held by the university libraries of Birmingham, Cambridge, London (Senate House), Rochester NY (Eastman School of Music, Sibley Music Library), Sheffield, Virginia (University of Virginia at Charlottesville) and Warwick, and by the following institutions: Royal Birmingham Conservatoire; the Rowe Music Library, King's College, Cambridge; the National Library of Scotland, Edinburgh; the British Library, the National Art Library (Victoria & Albert Museum) and the Royal Academy of Music, London; the University of Birmingham Shakespeare Institute, Stratford-upon-Avon; the Folger Shakespeare Library and the Library of Congress, Washington DC.

Finally, my thanks go to Simon P. Keefe and Catherine Anne Bradley, former and current series editors of Royal Musical Association Monographs, to my anonymous peer reviewers, to Peter Jones for polishing the music examples, and to Reji Baiju, Heidi Bishop, Stephanie Hines and especially Lillian Woodall for their helpful guidance during the process of publication. Needless to say, I take full responsibility for the errors and shortcomings that are likely to be found in this wide-ranging study.

Colin Timms
November 2023

Introduction

Exton Hall, Rutland, has a place in music history thanks to the productions of a version of Milton's *Comus* that were mounted there in 1745 and 1748 by Baptist Noel, 4th Earl of Gainsborough. In 1745 Handel stayed at the Hall as a guest and composed the masque's finale, consisting of a song for each of three singers and a chorus for all three, repeated after each song in the manner of a refrain. The entertainment also included ten movements from works that he had written during the previous two decades, and probably some numbers from Thomas Augustine Arne's setting of John Dalton's adaptation of *Comus*, which had opened at the Drury Lane theatre in 1738 and moved to Covent Garden in 1744. At Exton Handel may also have played the 'extempore Allegro' that marked the dramatic climax of the work and could conceivably have directed the performance of the entire entertainment from the keyboard. In 1748 the masque was staged outdoors in an elaborate garden theatre, specially constructed for the occasion, and the leading roles were taken by Lord Gainsborough and members of his family, including some of his children; the only outsider known to have taken part is John Randall, then organist of King's College, Cambridge, who played a Bacchanal (tenor). On the following day there was a performance of *Deborah* in the morning and a repeat performance of *Comus* in the evening, followed by supper and fireworks.[1]

These events did not pass unnoticed. On 13 July 1745 Mrs Margaret Smith, wife of the Member of Parliament (MP) for Leicestershire, wrote as follows to Miss Philippa Gee, who later became the second wife of Sir Edmund Isham, 6th Baronet Lamport and MP for Northamptonshire:

> we have had a great Deal of Entertainment in the Musickal way, by Mr Handels having been this Summer at Ld Gainsbro's, he was so complaisant as to compose three Songs, wch were introduce'd in ye Masque of Comus, wch was Perform'd there upon [remainder lost].[2]

Mrs Smith also described the entertainments given in 1748, writing on 31 August:

2 Introduction

I must not omit mentioning Exton, where tho there is no Wedings going forward that I hear of there is as much Gayity as wou'd serve for Twenty; their whole time is Dedicated to one continue'd Series of Pleasure; Plays acted both in the House, & in the Gardens, Musick, Fireworks, & Illuminations, & indeed every thing that can contribute towards Killing, or (I believe to Speak more Properly one shou'd say) making Time Glide insensibly away. at first no company was admitted to their Plays, but I believe now most of the Country [i.e., neighbourhood] has been there, tho' I have not been of ye Number, but I was at one of their Oratorios wch was very well Perform'd.[3]

Mrs Smith did not attend the plays, did not see *Comus* and, perhaps because Handel was not present in 1748, did not even mention that the masque had been produced. She did, however, hear 'one of their oratorios', and it was doubtless during this visit that she heard about the fireworks and illuminations. It is unfortunate that she did not identify any of the oratorios or record the number of performances.

From the secondary literature on Handel it appears that the entertainments at Exton in 1745 and 1748 were isolated events, but if one digs more deeply, a different picture emerges. In earlier letters Mrs Smith refers to theatrical productions in the summers of 1741 and 1742,[4] and a performance in 1741 is recorded also by Sybil Rosenfeld.[5] Neither writer gives details. According to Jenny Clark, who catalogued the Noel family papers in the Record Office for Leicestershire, Leicester and Rutland (hereinafter ROLLR), one of Lord Gainsborough's relations tried his or her hand at writing theatrical works, and a play about fox-hunting was acted by family members, among them Gainsborough's cousin Sherard Manners (c. 1713–42).[6] Furthermore, Gerard Noel maintains that 'summer concerts and festivals of music were a feature of life at Exton' and describes 'a week-long programme of musical events' in the late summer of 1750.[7]

Both Clark and Noel drew on the collection in ROLLR (catalogue reference D3214), which relates to the history of the Noel family at Exton Hall and includes documents pertaining

> to every aspect of the estate, including repairs and improvements to the property and gardens, manuring, harvest suppers, foxhounds and a stable of hunters, the purchase of plants, trees, provisions, wine, books, paintings, sculptures, and the cost of elections and funerals.[8]

This collection is the source of the twenty-one documents relating mainly to music, books and theatre that are transcribed and presented in Appendix II below. These documents shed new light on the artistic patronage of the 4th Earl of Gainsborough and thus increase our knowledge and understanding of the background to his productions of *Comus*.

Notes

1 Information on *Comus* at Exton was first published in Betty Matthews, 'Unpublished Letters concerning Handel', *Music & Letters*, 40 (1959), 261–8. These letters are also transcribed, along with a contemporary cue sheet found later by Anthony Hicks, in *George Frideric Handel: Collected Documents*, ed. Donald Burrows, Helen Coffey, John Greenacombe and Anthony Hicks, 6 vols. (Cambridge: Cambridge University Press, 2013–), iv, 322–7 and 588–90. Handel's finale was discovered by Hicks and edited by him and Colin Timms as Handel, *Music for 'Comus'* (London: Acca Music, 1977). The words and music of the complete masque were reconstructed by Timms as George Frideric Handel and Thomas Augustine Arne, *Comus* (London: Novello, 2016) and are discussed by him in 'Handel and *Comus* at Exton', in *New Perspectives on Handel's Music: Essays in Honour of Donald Burrows*, ed. David Vickers (Woodbridge: Boydell, 2022), 244–66.
2 London, British Library, Add. MS 29601, ff. 218–19, at 219v. See also *Handel: Collected Documents*, iv, 328–9, and David Hunter, 'Handel at Exton, Rutland', *Handel Institute Newsletter*, 25/1 (2014), [6–7].
3 Add. MS 29601, ff. 266–7, at 266v–267r. See also *Handel: Collected Documents*, iv, 594.
4 Hunter, 'Handel at Exton', [6].
5 Sybil Rosenfeld, *Temples of Thespis: Some Private Theatres and Theatricals in England and Wales, 1700–1820* (London: Society for Theatre Research, 1978), 172.
6 The amateur plays were *Amphitheatria, or Majesty in Liquor* and its sequel *The Wedding of Weddings, or Limberhambus Noos'd*: see Jenny Clark, 'Exton and the Noel Family', *Rutland Record*, 19 (1999), 397.
7 Gerard Noel, *Sir Gerard Noel MP and the Noels of Chipping Campden and Exton* (Chipping Campden: Campden and District Historical and Archaeological Society, 2004), 46.
8 Jenny Clark, 'Family Annals: The Exton Manuscripts', *Rutland Record*, 13 (1993), 120. A description of the collection can be found via http://record-office-catalogue.leics.gov.uk (accessed 18 July 2023). See also Historical Manuscripts Commission, GB-0056-DE3214: 'Summary Report on the Estate and Family Papers, 12th–20th Century, of the Noel Family, Earls of Gainsborough' (online: accessed 11 July 2023). The collection on deposit in ROLLR is owned by the Noel family; publication of photographs of the documents is not allowed.

1 The 4th Earl of Gainsborough

Baptist Noel belonged to a family that had come to England after the Norman conquest and flourished first in Staffordshire.[1] The branch of which he was a member originated with James Noel of Hilcote, Justice of the Peace for Staffordshire in the early sixteenth century, and rose to prominence with his third son, Andrew (d. 1562), who acquired the preceptory of Dalby-on-the-Wolds (Leicestershire) and the manors of Perrybar (Staffordshire) and Brooke (Rutland).[2] Andrew's son, another Andrew (d. 1607), married Mabel, daughter of Sir James Harington of Exton, was knighted in 1585 and died a wealthy man. In 1614 Exton Hall was sold by the Haringtons to Sir Baptist Hicks, a prosperous London merchant, later Viscount Campden. When Hicks died, in 1629, Exton and his other estates in Rutland, Gloucestershire and London passed via his elder daughter, Juliana, to her husband, Sir Edward Noel, son of Andrew and Mabel.[3] Exton Hall became the Noel family's principal seat in the mid-1640s, after their house in Chipping Campden had been ruined by fire during the Civil War. Edward was created Earl of Gainsborough in 1682, and his great-grandson Baptist became the fourth holder of the title, in 1714.

Baptist Noel was born on 23 May 1708 and baptised at Exton on 8 June; he was the first of six children – three boys and three girls. His mother Dorothy, a daughter of John Manners, 1st Duke of Rutland, was twenty-six years old; his father, also named Baptist, was a little younger but died early, on 17 April 1714.[4] His son was under six years of age when he succeeded his father as 4th Earl of Gainsborough, 4th Baron Noel of Titchfield, 6th Baron Noel of Ridlington, 7th Viscount Campden and 7th Baron Hicks of Ilmington. He was educated at Eton College and at St John's College, Cambridge, where he was admitted a fellow-commoner on 26 February 1724, at the age of fifteen. As was usual for sons of gentlemen at the time, he probably studied for a couple of years and left without taking a degree;[5] unlike many of his peers, he is not known to have undertaken a Grand Tour. In 1728 he married Elizabeth Chapman, the beautiful daughter of 'a yeoman farmer of Exton village'.[6] For a young man of his standing this was a most unconventional match, one born of love rather than desire for additional status or wealth. Gainsborough's union with 'the cottage countess' – the nickname by which his wife became known – produced thirteen children, of whom a son and two daughters died in infancy and another daughter at the age of ten:[7]

Elizabeth: baptised 10 October 1731 at Greenwich; died (unmarried) 27 November 1801 at Ketton (Rutland); buried at Exton

Jane: born 14 May, baptised 2 June 1733 in the parish of St Mary-la-Bonne (i.e., Marylebone; Middlesex); married Gerard Anne Edwards 8 October 1754; died 1811

Juliana: born 16 January, baptised 17 February 1735 at Exton; married George Evans, 3rd Baron Carbery, 7 February 1760; died in childbed 18 December 1760

Penelope: born 1736; died in infancy

Anne: born 18 September, baptised 20 October 1737 in the parish of St James, Westminster; died (unmarried) at North Luffenham (Rutland) in September 1825

Mary: born 11 January, baptised 8 February 1739 at Exton; died in infancy

Baptist: born 8 June, baptised 12 July 1740 at Greenwich; died (unmarried) 27 May 1759 in Geneva. 5th Earl of Gainsborough, no issue: the title passed to his brother Henry

Lucy: born 25 July, baptised 29 August 1741 at Exton; married Sir Horatio Mann MP, 2nd Baronet of Egerton, 1765; died in Italy

Henry: born 19 April, baptised 23 May 1743 at Exton; died (unmarried) 8 April 1798; buried 21 April. 6th Earl of Gainsborough, no issue: left Rutland estates to his nephew Gerard Noel Edwards (son of Jane), who immediately assumed the name Noel

Mary: baptised 13 May 1744 at Exton; living at North Luffenham in 1803; died 1820

Charles: baptised 16 April 1745 at Exton; buried two days later

Catharine-Susanna: baptised 13 February 1748 at Exton; buried 15 April 1758 at Exton

Sophia: born 24 March, baptised 25 April 1750 at Exton; married Christopher Nevile 1773; died 5 May 1780 at Wellingore, Lincolnshire; buried 15 May at nearby Aubourn.

After the birth of six daughters, the arrival of Gainsborough's first son – on 8 June 1740 at his house in Blackheath – was an occasion for great rejoicing, as the press was eager to report:

> Yesterday the Lady of the Right Hon. the Earl of Gainsborough was safely deliver'd of a Son, at his Lordship's House upon Blackheath; and in the Evening all the Tradesmen employ'd by his Lordship in Greenwich met at the Black Lyon to express their Joy upon that Occasion.[8]

Gainsborough must have been doubly delighted that his first son was born on 8 June, because this was the anniversary of his own baptism; doubtless it was also the date of the 'anniversary festival' on which the first Exton performance of *Comus* took place five years later.[9] By then only three of Gainsborough's five siblings were still alive – his sisters Catherine (1709–79)[10] and Susanna (1710–58), who in 1724 had married Anthony Ashley Cooper, 4th Earl of Shaftesbury, and his unmarried brother James (1712–52), MP for Rutland from 1734. Gainsborough died on 21 March 1751, leaving £6,000 to each of his eight surviving daughters, a 'provision' for his second son, and a wife big with child:

> The late Earl of Gainsborough has charged his estate with 6000 l. Portions to each of his eight Daughters, beside a Provision for his second son. The Countess of Gainsborough is pretty far advanced in her Pregnancy of the eleventh Child.[11]

The funeral took place on the Exton estate, in the parish church of St Peter and St Paul, and cost over £300.[12]

Having succeeded to the earldom as a young boy, Gainsborough grew into a devoted husband and father with an ambition to put his title and family more firmly on the map. This is eloquently demonstrated by the fact that in the mid-1730s he commissioned full-length portraits of five of his most illustrious Noel ancestors and one of himself (see Figure 1.1).[13] His own portrait is the only one that is signed and dated: the signatory is the little-known artist J. Henesy, the date 1737, and the likeness bears a striking resemblance to that in the engraving by John Faber junior, believed to be based on a portrait by Hans Hysing (1678–1752/3).[14] Gainsborough was in his late twenties when Henesy painted his portrait: adorned in his robes of peerage, he comes across as a very self-possessed young man. Around the same time he also commissioned Henesy to paint a family portrait of himself, his wife and their first three daughters – Elizabeth, Jane and Juliana.[15] The resulting work is an early example of a conversation piece, an 'informal small-scale portrait in domestic surroundings, the figures [...] disposed in an easy familiarity'.[16] This relatively new genre came into favour in the 1730s 'amongst People of fashion – even some of ye Royal Family'; among the most successful exponents, apart from Hogarth, were Gawen Hamilton (*c.* 1697–1737) and Charles Philips (1703–47). That Gainsborough commissioned such a painting shows that he was aware of the fashion and wanted his family to be associated with it: he was proud of his position in society and keen to record and project the image of his house.

Gainsborough's ambition is demonstrated also by his improvements to the Exton estate. He extended the family home (which dated from the late sixteenth century), redesigned the gardens and improved the parkland and farms. The expansion and development of the estate over the seventeenth and eighteenth centuries are illustrated by several images and plans.[17] An engraving of *c.* 1739 by John Harris (Figure 1.2) offers a bird's-eye view, with a side elevation of the Hall in the middle distance and the church close by. The

Figure 1.1 Baptist Noel, 4th Earl of Gainsborough. Portrait by J. Henesy, signed and dated 1737. Reproduced by kind permission of Sotheby's.

gardens and park are laid out in formal if not regular patterns. There is a substantial number and variety of trees, a great deal of manicured hedging, a lake and a pond (to the right) and in the foreground what appears to be some kind of maze. Animals and birds abound. At the front of the house (top left) dogs, horses and riders return from (or prepare for) a hunt; behind the house (middle-ground, right) there is a deer park; the lake below is home to ducks and

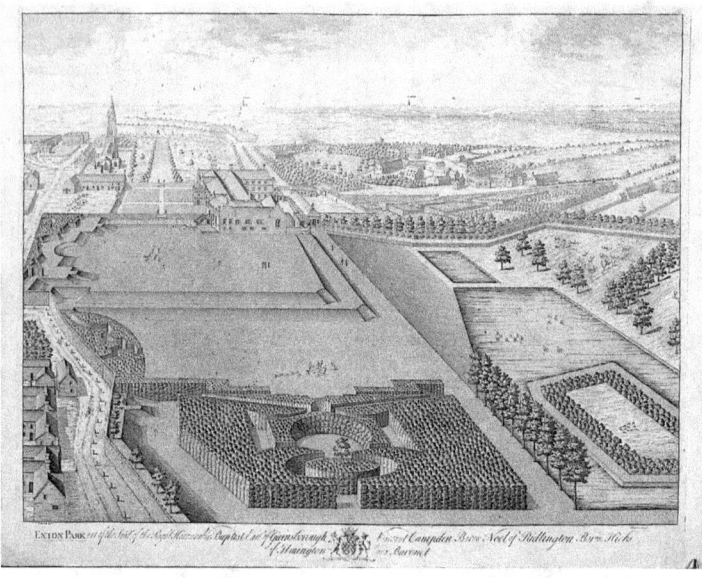

Figure 1.2 Exton Park. Engraving by John Harris (*c.* 1739) after a painting by Thomas Badeslade. © The British Library Board, Maps K.Top.36.6.1.b.

swans, and in the centre (foreground) what appear to be peacocks are accompanied by a number of ladies. In general, however, the ladies and gentlemen dotted around are made to appear less significant than their surroundings.

A different impression is conveyed by James Mason's engraving of *c.* 1749 (Figure 1.3), which gives a close-up view of part of the estate at ground level. By this time significant alterations had been made. The land is no longer so flat; the trees do not stand in serried ranks; the Hall – again a side elevation – is to the right, and there is a waterfall emptying into a new lake near the house, with people in a boat. There are more people elsewhere – two in the foreground (at least one on horseback) and eight in the middle ground (five to the left, four of them mounted, and three right of centre) – and they are depicted more prominently than in the earlier engraving. A group of what seem to be deer can be seen halfway up the slope on the left. The garden appears relatively natural and evokes the approach to design associated with Lancelot 'Capability' Brown (1716–83).[18] During the 1740s, the years between these two views of Exton, Brown was head gardener at Stowe (Buckinghamshire), and in 1750 Gainsborough purchased some 'views of Lrd Cobhams Gardens' and a copy of William Gilpin's *Dialogue upon the Gardens* [...] *at Stow* (1748, or second edition 1749).[19] Taken together with Mason's engraving, these purchases

Figure 1.3 Exton Park. Engraving by James Mason (*c.* 1749) after a painting by Thomas Smith. © The British Library Board, Maps K.Top.36.6.1.c.

suggest that Gainsborough admired the 1st Viscount Cobham's gardens at Stowe and sought to emulate them at Exton.[20]

As a peer of the realm the 4th Earl also owned property in London and performed a range of public duties. His daughter Anne was born in September 1737 at his house in Pall Mall, and according to Gerard Noel he also owned a mansion in Chandos Street, just off Cavendish Square.[21] The house in Blackheath where his son was born in 1740 had been bought in late May 1731:

> We hear that the Earl of Gainsborough has purchas'd of Col. Disney the House in Blackheath, late Lieutenant General Withers, deceased; and on Thursday last his Lordship entered upon the Premisses accordingly.[22]

When Colonel Disney died, six months later, Gainsborough benefited from the reversion of an annuity:

> by the Death of Col. Disney, an Annuity of 300 l. per Annum reverts to the Earl of Gainsborough, his Lordship having engag'd himself to pay the Colonel that Sum Yearly during his Life, as one Part of the Consideration for his fine House at Black Heath.[23]

On Saturday 31 January 1730 the *Newcastle Courant* reported that 'the Right Honourable Baptist Noel Earl of Gainsborough took the Oaths, and his seat in the House [of Peers]'; he was twenty-one at the time. In 1732 he became Lord Lieutenant of the county of Rutland, and in 1745 he held in his gift several clerical positions in Chipping Campden, Pickwell (Leicestershire), Exton, Horsfield ('united to Exton'), Whitwell and Ridlington (Rutland), and Seaham in County Durham.[24] The *Whitehall Evening Post or London Intelligencer* of 21–23 May 1747 reported that 'this Morning the Right Hon. the Earl of Gainsborough went out of Town with a large Retinue, and three Coaches and Six', while subsequent issues of the paper noted that in mid-March 1749 he 'took his Seat in the House of Peers' and two weeks later 'went out of Town to his Lordship's Seat at Exton'.[25]

An attractive picture of the interior of Exton Hall and its furnishings is painted by Gerard Noel on the basis of an inventory drawn up in 1717, just a few years after Gainsborough had succeeded to the title.[26] According to this document, many of the walls were hung with prints, drawings or paintings:[27]

Bellcony [balcony] Closset	27 prints and drawings
Closset over my Ladys appartment	1 picture
Little Dineing Roome	28 fine prints
Great Stairs Case	28 prints and 4 drawings
Great Dineing Roome	'family pieces' [paintings]
Best Drawing Roome	paintings
Great Hall	'15 Pieces of Family Paintings'
	'8 Pieces of Family Paintings'
	'1 Great piece of Painting of a Horse'
	'1 Great Clock with Pallasadoes about'
My Ladys Closset	'9 Prints in the Roome'

During the 1730s and 1740s, in common with such contemporaries as Charles Jennens and the 3rd Duke of Rutland, Gainsborough bought many more pictures for his houses in London and the country.[28] He is not regarded by art historians as a major collector,[29] but during these decades he acquired works 'by [Paolo] Veronese, Old Griffier, [Peter] Lely, Alberti, Baptista, [Gian Paolo] Panini, Agnese, Horizonti, Vandervelde and Hans Hyssing [Hysing]'; he also purchased etchings from Joseph Goupy and sculptures from Peter Scheemakers, and engaged Sefferin Alken to carve picture frames and chimneypieces for his houses.[30] Most of these artists are known and were represented in other eighteenth-century collections: Handel, for example, owned works by 'Old Griffier' (Jan Griffier the Elder (*c*. 1645–1718)), Panini, Horizonti and Goupy,[31] and in 1744 the Duke of Rutland paid Jan Griffier the Younger (1688–*c*. 1750) for a *View of Belvoir Castle*.[32] 'Vandervelde' could be a reference to Willem van der Velde the Elder (1611–93) or his son Willem the Younger (1633–1707) – or even to his grandson, another Willem. The

Fleming Peter Scheemakers was one of the most successful sculptors in mid-eighteenth-century England, while the young Danish sculptor Sefferin Alken, born in 1717, appears to have come to London in 1744. 'Alberti', 'Baptista' and 'Agnese' have not been identified.

Some evidence of Gainsborough's interest in pictures is found among the Noel family papers in ROLLR. According to one bill, he paid for pictures to be transported by cart in July 1744, apparently to London, and in December 1744 and January 1745 to Wood Street in an unspecified town or city; in 1745 he paid for the stretching of frames and for 'Cleaning. Mending & Beautifying Eight Pictures. whereof one was a Whole Length'.[33] The recipient of £21 2s. 10d. for all these services was James Bonus, who was also paid £24 5s. 0d. 'in full of all Demands' in August 1746.[34] On 1 April 1747 Gainsborough paid 'Mr Lambe' £39 1s. 6d. for five lots of pictures, bought in a sale.[35] The auctioneer was presumably Aaron Lambe, whose 'Great Auction Room' was situated in Pall Mall.[36] It appears that each lot consisted of a single work, for on 29 May Gainsborough paid £2 12s. 0d. for 'Five Packing Cases & Packing ye Pictures'.[37] The documents do not identify the works or the artists, and the pertinent sale catalogue has not come to light, but since Lot 62 went for £22 1s. 0d., it must have been very large or desirable.

The 'whole-length' picture mentioned above could have been the full-length portrait of Gainsborough's wife or their son, both of which were commissioned by the earl from Arthur Pond (1701–58).[38] Pond visited Italy in 1725–7 with the painter George Knapton, among others, and by the mid-1730s had become a fashionable portrait artist, particularly in crayons. He also became an engraver and a dealer in prints, and was recognised as an art connoisseur. In the 1740s he helped produce illustrations for Thomas Birch's *Heads of Illustrious Persons of Great Britain*, published by John and Paul Knapton, to which Gainsborough subscribed.[39] In view of the two commissioned portraits and this subscription, one might expect Pond's manuscript 'Journal of Receipts & Expenses from 1734–1750' to include evidence of further dealings with the earl, but Gainsborough's name appears only twice in the ledger: on 3 June 1748 he was billed 2s. 6d. for 'Anson' – an entry that must be related to his purchase that month of either the anonymous account of George Anson's *Voyage to the South-Seas* or a print of the distinguished seaman – and on 11 March 1749 he was charged the same amount for a cart, possibly for the transport of a work of art.[40]

In all these respects Gainsborough seems to have been a typical eighteenth-century English peer: as Mark Girouard explains, during the seventeenth and eighteenth centuries 'it became more and more important for a gentleman to be cultivated as well as literate. Culture became an essential part of the image of a worthy ruling class'.[41] Nevertheless, Gainsborough seems to have been exceptionally cultivated, interested in a wide variety of subjects and active in his pursuit of them. John Skynner, a fellow of St John's College, Cambridge, who preached the sermon at his funeral, extolled his many admirable qualities but drew special attention to his intellectual and artistic interests and to his humanity and conviviality:[42]

> The hospitality of his temper was extremely remarkable, and well worthy that diffusive spirit of benevolence, which was once the general (and would to God it had been the constant) characteristic of our British gentry and nobles. No guest ever entered his mansion who was not received with all the warmth of the most generous welcome; and many can witness, that they seldom, if ever, knew any one return from thence within the time limited for his departure. It was indeed the great and enlarged pleasure of the deceased, to see his house perpetually filled with his friends, and to detain them in it by all the polite and manly amusements, that could engage them to prolong their visit. [...] His skill in musick, painting, and poetry; his knowledge in the principal arts and embellishments of elegant life; to which I may add a very judicious acquaintance with history, and the sciences, rendered him at all times capable of furnishing out a refined entertainment both for himself, and others, of the same improved and cultivated taste.

During Gainsborough's maturity, at least, Exton Hall seems to have been a 'social house'.[43] The countess must have been very pleased with Skynner's affectionate remarks on her late husband, rewarding him handsomely for his sermon with the sum of twenty guineas.[44]

Subscriptions to Books and Music

Assuming that Skynner eschewed flattery and exaggeration, the foundations of Gainsborough's 'knowledge in the principal arts' and 'acquaintance with history, and the sciences' were presumably laid during his periods at Eton and Cambridge.[45] The young earl could have built on them, however, by reading at home in Exton. When the Hall was inventoried in 1717, it housed '1 Great Press for Bookes'.[46] He was only eight or nine years old at that time, but from 1725 to 1750 he subscribed to the publication of books on a variety of subjects. The list in Appendix I, below, may be incomplete and therefore somewhat misleading, but it is interesting to see, nevertheless, that in addition to Boccaccio in Italian (with a dedication signed by Paolo Rolli [1725]), Castiglione in parallel Italian and English (1727 and 1742) and a translation of Homer (1726) – along with works on horse-racing (1729),[47] history (1732–5 and 1750), husbandry (1733), law (1738) and 'natural philosophy' (1748) – he subscribed to a volume of portraits engraved by Houbraken (1743) and to several volumes of English literature, notably poetry (1725, 1726, 1748 and 1749), and was the dedicatee of a book on the therapeutic effects of music (1729) – a fact of particular interest in the context of this study.

The Noel family appears to have been interested in music for well over a century before Baptist acceded to the earldom, as well as during his lifetime. At Brooke House there were virginals in the dining chamber and in another room, and 'a pair of wind instruments at the stair head'.[48] When Exton Hall was inventoried in 1717, the surveyors found 'one Set of Organs' in the organ loft and '7 Basses and Covers to them' in the chapel gallery.

Gainsborough himself, as Appendix I makes clear, subscribed to at least two publications of music in the 1720s, three in the 1730s and four in the 1740s. He may have been only sixteen years old when he subscribed to the publication in 1724 of six cantatas and six lessons for viola d'amore by Attilio Ariosti, one of the composers of Italian opera for the Royal Academy of Music. Ariosti dedicated his volume to King George I and used the heading of the dedication as the title of the work: *Alla Maestà di Giorgio Rè della Gran Bretagna*. He attracted an exceptionally long list of 763 subscribers, including over forty dukes and duchesses, six marquises, 115 earls and countesses, 115 lords and ladies and over fifty knights and ladies; he also identified 132 of his supporters as subscribers to the Royal Academy. Irrespective of any interest in Ariosti or his music, the young Gainsborough knew that his name had to be in that list.[49] In the following year both he and his mother, the dowager countess, subscribed to a collection of arias from operas by Handel, Bononcini and Ariosti (*A Pocket Companion for Gentlemen and Ladies*), suggesting that the family was (or wanted to be) familiar with the most popular numbers in the Royal Academy's productions.

Having married in 1728, Gainsborough and his wife, the Countess, subscribed independently to Michael Christian Festing's *Twelve Sonatas in Three Parts*, op. 2 (1731: see Figure 1.4).[50] She had already been a subscriber to his *Twelve Solo's for a Violin and Thorough Bass*, op. 1 (1730), and her husband was to subscribe to the composer's *Six Solos for a Violin and Thorough-Bass*, op. 7 [1747]. These three subscriptions suggest that chamber music, especially for stringed instruments, played an important part in the musical life of the Noels and, more particularly, that some members of the family may have been acquainted with Festing, who was a violinist as well as a composer. The former impression is reinforced by the earl's subscription to Charles Maclean's *Twelve Solo's or Sonatas for a Violin and Violoncello, with a Thorough Bass for Harpsichord*, op. 1 (1737), John Hebden's *Six Concertos in Seven Parts*, op. 2 [1745] and William Boyce's *Twelve Sonatas for two Violins, with a Bass for the Violoncello or Harpsicord* (1747). Meanwhile, Gainsborough had also subscribed to two more editions of vocal music – George Bickham's *The Musical Entertainer*, vol. 1 (1737) and Musgrave Heighington's *Six Select Odes of Anacreon in Greek and Six of Horace in Latin* [1745].[51] Vocal works account for slightly less than half of the editions to which he subscribed; indeed, during the period in question, 1724 to 1747, the emphasis gradually shifted from vocal music to instrumental.

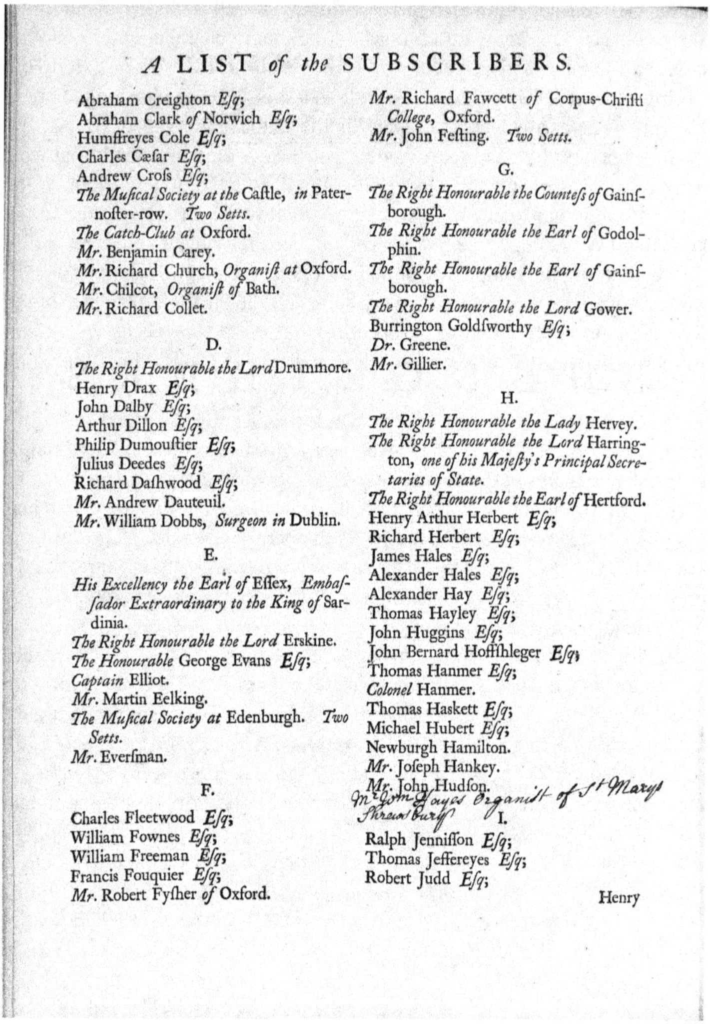

A LIST of the SUBSCRIBERS.

Abraham Creighton *Esq*;
Abraham Clark *of* Norwich *Esq*;
Humffreyes Cole *Esq*;
Charles Cæsar *Esq*;
Andrew Crofs *Esq*;
The *Musical Society at the* Castle, *in* Paternoster-row. *Two Setts.*
The *Catch-Club at* Oxford.
Mr. Benjamin Carey.
Mr. Richard Church, *Organist at* Oxford.
Mr. Chilcot, *Organist of* Bath.
Mr. Richard Collet.

D.

The *Right Honourable the Lord* Drummore.
Henry Drax *Esq*;
John Dalby *Esq*;
Arthur Dillon *Esq*;
Philip Dumoustier *Esq*;
Julius Deedes *Esq*;
Richard Dashwood *Esq*;
Mr. Andrew Dauteuil.
Mr. William Dobbs, *Surgeon in* Dublin.

E.

His *Excellency the Earl of* Essex, *Embassador Extraordinary to the King of* Sardinia.
The *Right Honourable the Lord* Erskine.
The *Honourable* George Evans *Esq*;
Captain Elliot.
Mr. Martin Eelking.
The *Musical Society at* Edenburgh. *Two Setts.*
Mr. Eversman.

F.

Charles Fleetwood *Esq*;
William Fownes *Esq*;
William Freeman *Esq*;
Francis Fouquier *Esq*;
Mr. Robert Fysher *of* Oxford.

Mr. Richard Fawcett *of* Corpus-Christi *College,* Oxford.
Mr. John Festing. *Two Setts.*

G.

The *Right Honourable the Countess of* Gainsborough.
The *Right Honourable the Earl of* Godolphin.
The *Right Honourable the Earl of* Gainsborough.
The *Right Honourable the Lord* Gower.
Burrington Goldsworthy *Esq*;
Dr. Greene.
Mr. Gillier.

H.

The *Right Honourable the Lady* Hervey.
The *Right Honourable the Lord* Harrington, *one of his Majesty's Principal Secretaries of State.*
The *Right Honourable the Earl of* Hertford.
Henry Arthur Herbert *Esq*;
Richard Herbert *Esq*;
James Hales *Esq*;
Alexander Hales *Esq*;
Alexander Hay *Esq*;
Thomas Hayley *Esq*;
John Huggins *Esq*;
John Bernard Hofsthleger *Esq*;
Thomas Hanmer *Esq*;
Colonel Hanmer.
Thomas Haskett *Esq*;
Michael Hubert *Esq*;
Newburgh Hamilton.
Mr. Joseph Hankey.
Mr. John Hudson.
Mr. John Hayes *Organist of St Marys Shrewsbury*

I.

Ralph Jennisson *Esq*;
Thomas Jeffereyes *Esq*;
Robert Judd *Esq*;

Henry

Figure 1.4 Michael Christian Festing, *Twelve Sonatas in Three Parts* [...] *Opera secunda* (London: Printed by William Smith [...] and Sold only by the Author, 1731). Part of the list of subscribers. Reproduced by kind permission of the Syndics of Cambridge University Library.

There could be many reasons why Gainsborough subscribed to publications of music, but there can be little doubt that he was genuinely interested in the art. His 'skill in music', mentioned at his funeral, had already been referred to over twenty years earlier in Richard Browne's *Medicina Musica: or, A Mechanical Essay on the Effects of Singing, Musick, and Dancing, on Human Bodies* (1729), of which he was the dedicatee. This book is a revised and corrected edition of Browne's *Mechanical Essay on Singing, Musick, and Dancing* (1727), which 'was not wrote in a Frolick, but upon a serious Consideration of the manifold Advantages that may accrue to us from such Divertisements'.[52] The title page of *Medicina Musica* states that, for this later edition, the author had added 'a new essay on the nature and cure of the spleen and vapours' (see Figure 1.5). It also describes Browne as an 'apothecary in Oakham, in the county of Rutland', and the publisher John Cooke as a bookseller in Uppingham, a town about ten miles from Exton. As an apothecary, Browne may easily have become acquainted with Gainsborough and his family at Exton, only five miles from Oakham. Through its author, publisher and dedicatee *Medicina Musica* was firmly rooted in the area where the Noels' country seat was located.

Browne begins his dedication by congratulating Gainsborough on reaching the age of twenty-one:

> My Lord, I Think myself extremely happy in having the Honour of being the first in an Address to your Lordship, at a time when Duty requires my Congratulations upon your Lordship's Arrival at the Age, which admits you to all the Privileges of your high Birth and Peerage, and places you in Publick Life.

This introductory sentence is followed immediately by a compliment on Gainsborough's attitude to study:

> Your Lordship is well known to have employ'd the time of your Minority in a commendable Application to all the Parts of polite and useful Learning, and to have highly improv'd those Endowments with which Nature herself had happily enrich'd you.

Finally, Browne acknowledges Gainsborough's 'genius' for music and expresses the hope that his book, though concerned with music's effects on the body, will be of interest to its dedicatee:

> With regard to the small Treatise I here humbly offer to your Lordship, I have the Vanity to hope it may afford some Amusement to a Leisure Hour, as the Subjects of it are of a curious Nature, and such as fall in with your Lordship's distinguish'd Genius for Musick.

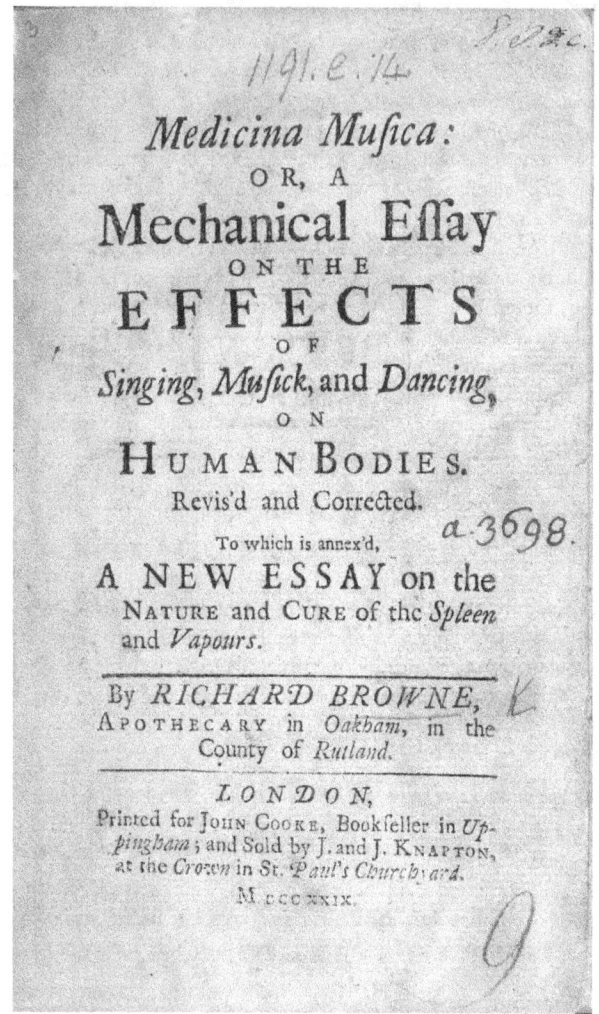

Figure 1.5 Richard Browne, *Medicina Musica: or, A Mechanical Essay on the Effects of Singing, Musick, and Dancing, on Human Bodies* […] (London: John Cooke, 1729). Title page. © The British Library Board, 1191.e.14.

The main thrust of Browne's book is that singing and dancing make physical demands, particularly on the lungs and the heart, and that this exercise benefits both the body and the mind, among other things helping cure the afflictions of 'spleen and vapours'. Music and dancing were widely regarded as desirable accomplishments and were included in the education of young men and women,[53] but Browne's belief in their therapeutic powers was evidently more far-reaching. According to Alicia Clair Gibbons and George N. Heller, *Medicina Musica* is

> a significant document in the history of music therapy and related fields because it was the first treatise in the English language to assert that success in music does not depend on proficiency attainable only by practiced [*sic*] musicians but rather on success at appropriate ability and function levels

and to argue that 'music has a wide variety of therapeutic applications' and 'may be used in preventive health care'.[54] The implication of Browne's dedication is that Gainsborough, with his 'distinguish'd Genius for Musick', was a singer as a boy and young man and was aware of the benefits that singing conferred. If he was, it would have been natural for him to insist that his (as yet unborn) children should sing. The fact that in *Comus*, in 1748, he and two of his daughters sang music by Handel – and possibly also danced – on stage in front of an audience suggests that this is precisely what he did.

Interests in music were cultivated also by Gainsborough's siblings. Both his brother James and his cousin Thomas Noel are listed among the subscribers to Maclean's *Twelve Solo's or Sonatas* in 1737. On 23 November 1739 James 'read through the whole Poem of [Milton's] Sampson Agonistes' to Handel and the 4th Earl of Shaftesbury,[55] apparently hoping to tempt the composer to use it as the basis of a new work, and on 12 January 1744 he subscribed to the composer's forthcoming London season,[56] which included the first performances of *Semele* and *Joseph and his Brethren* and revivals of *Samson* and *Saul*. He played the part of the Elder Brother in the production of *Comus* at Exton in 1748[57] and may have done the same three years earlier. Gainsborough's sister Susanna, Countess of Shaftesbury, was an ardent Handel supporter whose reactions to *Susanna* and *Theodora* display acumen and experience as a judge of music and drama.[58] And on 26 April 1746 their sister Catherine entertained Handel, Thomas Harris and others to dinner and supper at her house in London:[59] perhaps she had met the composer during the previous summer at Exton.

The earliest indication that Gainsborough might be interested in Handel is his subscription to *A Pocket Companion* in 1725, but the first piece of evidence that he may have been familiar with at least some of the composer's music is a letter of 22 April 1736 from Shaftesbury to his cousin James Harris, reminding him to let him have a copy of 'Tears such as tender fathers shed', from *Deborah* (1733), 'for me to send Lord Gainsborough & to write it in the manner we agreed upon'.[60] This lovely short air, which had not been published in Walsh's edition of the oratorio's *Songs* [1735],[61] is sung by Abinoam (bass) to his son, Barak, and accompanied by first and second violins, two transverse flutes, 'organi soft' and continuo. It is not known whether Gainsborough had asked Shaftesbury to send him a copy of the air or whether the latter had had the idea of sending it to his brother-in-law. Either way, the episode could be related to the birth and death, both in 1736, of Gainsborough's daughter Penelope. What Shaftesbury meant by 'write it in the manner we agreed upon' is uncertain, but the phrase presumably refers to changes to the air – perhaps to the words or the scoring – to make it appropriate to the family circumstances and/or suitable for a domestic performance.

It seems that Gainsborough and his family, when in London, attended musical performances directed by Handel. The documentary evidence to this effect is scanty but nevertheless persuasive. One indication is provided by a letter of 10 March 1747 from Mary Cantrell, sister of Reverend William Cantrell, of Exton, to Lady Jane Noel, Gainsborough's thirteen-year-old daughter, in London: 'I don't even, wish to partake of any of your diversion's but the Oratorios [...] I may be in London against Saturday Night'.[62] Mary may have been thinking of travelling to London in order to attend the performance of *Joseph and his Brethren* scheduled for 18 March; this was cancelled, but a performance was given two days later. Even if she did not make the journey, her phrase 'any of your diversion's but the Oratorios' suggests that Jane Noel, and possibly other members of the family, did attend these performances, perhaps on a regular basis. Two years later, on 17 March 1749, Gainsborough was charged 1s. 0d. by a stationer in London for a wordbook of 'Solomon an Oratorio';[63] since this is the date on which Handel's *Solomon* was first performed, it is reasonable to assume that at least one member of Gainsborough's family went to Covent Garden and heard it. Exactly the same can be said for the revival of *Messiah* on 23 March, when he was billed for two copies of the wordbook of that oratorio.[64]

By 1747, of course, Gainsborough was personally acquainted with Handel. When they first met is not known, but they must have had ample opportunity to get to know each other in June 1745, when the composer stayed at Exton as a guest and helped the family compile their version of *Comus*. When the masque was repeated in 1748, Benjamin Martyn informed Lord Shaftesbury that Gainsborough took the title role, 'spoke his Part excellently', and sang the bass air and the bass part of the trio in the finale that Handel had composed three years earlier.[65] It is probable, therefore, that Gainsborough had learned to read music notation and had sung as a boy or young man – as implied by Browne in the dedication of *Medicina Musica*. He is unlikely to have been able to make such prominent contributions as a singer and an actor in *Comus* if he had not previously received some grounding in the appropriate disciplines or gained some experience of performing.

Gainsborough's 'skill in musick' was accompanied, according to Skynner, by skill in painting and poetry. It is impossible now to confirm whether the earl possessed skill as a painter, because there are no known examples of his work, but there is evidence that he exercised a talent for poetry. He certainly was interested in poetry: his subscriptions to books make this clear, and he may have had a hand in the manuscript volume of poems described in Appendix II.18, which paints an appealing picture of the gardens at Exton and life at the Hall between 1745 and about 1752.

In addition, more than thirty years after his death Gainsborough was credited in print with the composition of the following poem:[66]

*By the Earl of Gainsborough**

The Persians stretch their votive arms
To Phoebus in his rising state;
I gaze on dear Myrtilla's charms,
And meet those eyes that dart my fate.

Example 1.1 F. Marchant, 'As Persians stretch their votive arms'. Transcription from a printed song sheet (c. 1730), bars 1–16.

Example 1.2 Anon., 'The Persians stretch their votive arms'. Transcription from British Library, Add. MS 31806, f. 20, bars 1–7.

> So the fond moth round tapers plays,
> Nor dreams of death in such bright fires:
> With joy he hastes into the blaze;
> He courts his doom, and there expires.

* *Baptist Noel, the fourth Earl*

The late date of publication might lead one to doubt the attribution, were it not for a setting of the poem for soprano and continuo on a printed songsheet, dated by the British Library to *c*. 1730. The song, beginning 'As [*sic*] Persians stretch their votive arms', is attributed to 'Marchand' (see Example 1.1). The British Library also possesses three other songs credited to 'Mr Marchand', and the heading to one of these (*c*. 1720) describes the composer as 'Organest to the Duke of Rutland'.[67] A servant named 'Mr Marchand' worked at Belvoir

Castle in the second half of 1713, at least: he was paid £10 at Christmas and signed his name as 'F. Marchant'.[68] Since Gainsborough was related by marriage to John Manners, who became 3rd Duke of Rutland in 1721 and took a practical interest in music, it seems possible that he really was the author of the words 'As Persians stretch their votive arms' that were set to music by Rutland's organist.

Another setting of the same poem – for four voices, apparently without accompaniment (see Example 1.2) – is preserved in British Library, Add. MS 31806, which dates from the late eighteenth and early nineteenth centuries. It would be gratifying if this work could be considered a product of Gainsborough's 'genius' for music, but there is no evidence that he was involved in its composition and the music may be too late in style to have been written before he died in 1751.

Notes

1 For fuller accounts of the history of the Noel family see: Emilia F. Noel, *Some Letters and Records of the Noel Family* (London: St Catherine Press, 1910); Jenny Clark, 'Family Annals: The Exton Manuscripts', *Rutland Record*, 13 (1993), 118–24, and 'Exton and the Noel Family', *Rutland Record*, 19 (1999), 382–99; Gerard Noel, *Sir Gerard Noel MP and the Noels of Chipping Campden and Exton* (Chipping Campden: Campden and District Historical and Archaeological Society, 2004), 17–47. See also the descriptions of the Noel papers, cited in the Introduction, note 8.
2 A view of Brooke House is published in Noel, *Some Letters and Records*, facing page 14.
3 For a list of Hicks's benefactions see Noel, *Some Letters and Records*, 11–12.
4 His passing was commemorated by Elkanah Settle's *Thalia lacrimans. A Funeral Poem to the Memory of the Right Honourable Baptist Earl of Gainsborough* (London: The Author, 1714).
5 This is the pattern that was followed by Charles Jennens at Oxford: see Ruth Smith, 'The Achievements of Charles Jennens (1700–73)', *Music & Letters*, 70 (1989), 173. For Baptist Noel see 'A Cambridge Alumni Database' – https://venn.lib.cam.ac.uk (accessed 18 July 2023). Noel does not appear in John Venn, *Alumni Cantabrigiensis: A Biographical List of all known Students, Graduates and Holders of Office at the University of Cambridge, from the Earliest Times to 1900*, vol. 1: *From the Earliest Times to 1751* (Cambridge: Cambridge University Press, 2011), and there is no article on him in the *Oxford Dictionary of National Biography Online*.
6 Noel, *Sir Gerard Noel MP*, 50. Her father, William Chapman, has also been described as a gamekeeper and a park-keeper.
7 This list is based mainly on Noel, *Some Letters and Records*, 23–4 and a genealogical table at the back of her book, and on Noel, *Sir Gerard Noel MP*, Appendix VI.
8 *The General Evening Post*, no. 1047, for 7–10 June 1740 (accessible online in Seventeenth and Eighteenth Century Burney Newspapers Collection).
9 Colin Timms, 'Handel and *Comus* at Exton', in *New Perspectives on Handel's Music: Essays in Honour of Donald Burrows*, ed. David Vickers (Woodbridge: Boydell, 2022), 244–66, at 250–51.
10 The date of Catherine's death was unknown to Emilia F. Noel. According to Thomas William Wake Smart, *A Chronology of Cranborne, being an Account of the ancient*

Town, Lordship, and Chase of Cranborne in the County of Dorset (London: Nichols and Sons, and others, 1841), 35, 'Lady Catherine Noel, obt, 15*th.*, Dec. 1779, is interred in the vault of Robert Prower, M.D.' in the parish church of St Mary and St Bartholomew. If this is the 'right' Catherine Noel, she may have moved to Cranborne to be close to her sister Susanna who, after marrying Lord Shaftesbury, lived at Wimborne St Giles, barely two miles away.

11 *The Remembrancer (1747)* for Saturday 6 April 1751 (Burney Newspapers). This infant must have died very young.
12 Clark, 'Family Annals', 120.
13 These ancestors were: Edward Noel (1582–1643), 2nd Viscount Campden; Baptist Noel (1612–82), 3rd Viscount Campden; Edward Noel (1641–89), 1st Earl of Gainsborough; Wriothesley Baptist Noel (*c*. 1661–90), 2nd Earl of Gainsborough, and Baptist Noel (1684–1714), 3rd Earl of Gainsborough. These five portraits, along with that of the 4th Earl and also a portrait of the 4th Earl as a young boy, formed part of the estate of the Hon. Thomas Noel (1958–2022). All of them were auctioned by Sotheby's on 5 April 2023 in a sale entitled 'Old Master & 19th Century Paintings' – the boy as Lot 85, the other six as Lot 87.
14 See Wilhelm Nisser, *Michael Dahl and the Contemporary Swedish School of Painting* (Uppsala: Almqvist & Wiksell, 1927), *103* [NB italic]. Faber's engraving is reproduced in Timms, 'Handel and *Comus* at Exton', 249.
15 This painting was auctioned on 24 January 2008 as Lot 334 in a Sotheby's sale entitled 'Important Old Master Paintings, including European Works of Art'. It is readily accessible online.
16 These remarks about conversation pieces are based on John Hayes, 'Introduction', in *Polite Society by Arthur Devis, 1712–1787: Portraits of the English Country Gentleman and his Family*, ed. Michael Cross (Preston: Harris Museum and Art Gallery, 1983), 9–16, at 9 and 14.
17 Views of the Old Hall and estate can be seen in: *A History of the County of Rutland*, ed. William Page, 2 vols. (London: Constable, 1908, and St Catherine Press, 1935), ii, frontispiece, and plate facing p. 128; Noel, *Some Letters and Records*, facing pp. 8 and 82; Clark, 'Exton and the Noel Family', 383 and 385, and 'Family Annals', 119; Noel, *Sir Gerard Noel MP*, 35.
18 See Roger Turner, *Capability Brown and the Eighteenth-Century English Landscape Garden* (London: Weidenfeld & Nicolson, 1985), and Michael Symes, *The English Landscape Garden: A Survey* (Swindon: Historic England, 2019).
19 See Appendix II.5, 10 July 1750.
20 When the estate was further landscaped in the later eighteenth century, it comprised 'some 1700 acres (700 hectares)': Leonard Cantor and Anthony Squires, *The Historic Parks and Gardens of Leicestershire and Rutland* (Newton Linford: Kairos Press, 1997), 57.
21 'Last Saturday Night the Right Hon. the Countess of Gainsborough was safely delivered of a Daughter, [at] the Earl's House in Pall-Mall', *Stamford Mercury*, Thursday 22 September 1737 (The British Newspaper Archive); Noel, *Sir Gerard Noel MP*, 45.
22 *The Daily Courant*, no. 9226, Monday 31 May 1731 (Burney Newspapers: see note 8).
23 *Read's Weekly Journal or British Gazetteer*, no. 349, Saturday 27 November 1731 (Burney Newspapers).
24 *The Clergyman's Intelligencer: or A Compleat Alphabetical List of all the Patrons in England and Wales, with the Dignities, Livings, and Benefices in their Gift; and their Valuations Annex'd* (London: J. and P. Knapton and others, 1745), 81.
25 *The Whitehall Evening Post, or London Intelligencer*, nos. 199, 483 and 488 (Burney Newspapers).
26 Noel, *Sir Gerard Noel MP*, 44–5.

27 This list is extracted from 'An Inventory of the Remine/ing part of the Goods in Exton House 1717': ROLLR, DE3214/8492.
28 Jennens started collecting in the 1730s, the 3rd Duke of Rutland in the 1740s: see Smith, 'The Achievements of Charles Jennens', 169–70, and Carole Taylor, 'John (Manners), 3rd Duke of Rutland: British Art Collector', *Journal of the History of Collections*, 29/2 (2017), 239–42.
29 For example, he does not appear in Thomas Martyn, *The English Connoisseur: Containing an Account of* [...] *Painting, Sculpture, &c. in the Palaces and Seats of the Nobility and Principal Gentry of England* (1766), 2nd edn (Dublin: T. and J. Whitehouse, 1767), James Stourton and Charles Sebag-Montefiore, *The British as Art Collectors: From the Tudors to the Present* (London: Scala, 2012) or Louise Lippincott, *Selling Art in Georgian London: The Rise of Arthur Pond* (London: Yale University Press, 1983).
30 Clark, 'Exton and the Noel Family' (see note 1), 384 and 387.
31 See Thomas McGeary, 'Handel as Art Collector: Art, Connoisseurship and Taste in Hanoverian Britain', *Early Music*, 37 (2009), 567–8.
32 See Taylor, 'John (Manners), 3rd Duke of Rutland', 244.
33 ROLLR, DE3214/10184/[1].
34 ROLLR, DE3214/10184/[2]. *Kent's Directory for the Year 1763* (London: Henry Kent, 1763), 18, mentions 'Bonus James, William & Thomas, Slop-sellers, *Thames-street*, near the Custom House'. In Thomas Mortimer, *The Universal Director; or, The Nobleman and Gentleman's True Guide to the Masters and Professors of the Liberal and Polite Arts and Sciences and of the Mechanic Arts, Manufactures, and Trades, Established in London and Westminster, and their Environs*, 2 vols. (London: J. Coote, 1763), Part III, 111, 'Bonus, John' is listed as a slop seller at the same address. 'John' could be a mistake.
35 ROLLR, DE3214/10184/[3]. Gainsborough bought Lot 5 for £2 18s. 0d., Lot 19 (£7 2s. 6d.), Lot 60 (£4 0s. 0d.), Lot 62 (£22 1s. 0d.) and Lot 87 (£3 0s. 0d.).
36 See, for example, *A Catalogue of Original Pictures lately consigned from Abroad, Out of the Galleries of the Two Brothers the Barons of Vicq, at Brussels and Brughes* [...] *To be sold by Auction, by Mr. Lambe, at his Great Auction Room in Pall Mall* [...]. This sale took place on 17 and 18 January 1749.
37 ROLLR, DE3214/10184/[4].
38 Clark, 'Exton and the Noel Family', 384 and 387. For a study of Pond see Lippincott, *Selling Art in Georgian London*.
39 See below, Appendix I, 1743.
40 Pond's 'Journal' is British Library, Add. MS 23724. The two 'Gainsborough' entries are found on ff. 153r and 162r, respectively. For Gainsborough's Anson-related purchases see Appendix II.5 (11 and 21 June 1748 and 17 July 1749) and II.7 (16 June 1748).
41 Mark Girouard, *Life in the English Country House* (New Haven: Yale University Press, 1978), 180.
42 John Skynner, *A Sermon preach'd at the Funeral of Baptist Earl of Gainsborough, April 18, 1751* (London: R. Dodsley, [1751]), 11–12.
43 'The Social House: 1720–70' is the title of Chapter 7 in Girouard, *Life in the English Country House*.
44 ROLLR, DE3214/5575/38.
45 For a brief summary of an upper-class boy's education see Richard Leppert, *Music and Image: Domesticity, Ideology and Socio-Cultural Formation in Eighteenth-Century England*, paperback edn (Cambridge: Cambridge University Press, 1993), 51. For further secondary literature on education see Chapter 2, note 10.
46 ROLLR, DE3214/8492.

47 Numerous references to Gainsborough's horses, dating from 1722 to 1740, can be found in the *Stamford Mercury* (The British Newspaper Archive). Three of his hunters were burned at Exton in November 1731 in a fire that damaged the stables: *The London Evening Post*, no. 619, 16–18 November 1731 (Burney Newspapers: see above, note 8).
48 Clark, 'Exton and the Noel Family', 384.
49 For a survey of music publishing by subscription in eighteenth-century Britain see *Music by Subscription: Composers and their Networks in the British Music-Publishing Trade, 1676–1820*, ed. Simon D. I. Fleming and Martin Perkins (London: Routledge, 2021). For discussion of Ariosti's list see p. 225.
50 Three editions of these sonatas appeared in 1731. An edition published by 'the Author' is preserved only at the Royal Academy of Music (London). Another, issued by John Johnson, survives in a single copy at the University of Sheffield. The third edition, which is held by several libraries, bears the imprint shown in Figure 1.4 and is the only one in which a list of subscribers appears.
51 Two editions of this work were published, in 1745 and 1747, respectively. Both include six settings of Anacreon but only three of Horace. The second edition provides a transliteration of the Greek texts: see *George Frideric Handel: Collected Documents*, ed. Donald Burrows, Helen Coffey, John Greenacombe and Anthony Hicks, 6 vols. (Cambridge: Cambridge University Press, 2013–), iv, 304, 307 and 310–11.
52 Richard Browne, *A Mechanical Essay on Singing, Musick and Dancing. Containing their Uses and Abuses; and demonstrating by Clear and Evident Reasons, the Alterations they produce in the Human Body* (London: J. Pemberton, 1727), Introduction, [p. 2].
53 See Leppert, *Music and Image*, especially Chapters 3, 4 and 5.
54 Gibbons, Alicia Clair, and George N. Heller, 'Music Therapy in Handel's England: Browne's *Medicina Musica* (1729)', *College Music Symposium*, 25 (1985), 72.
55 Shaftesbury to James Harris, 24 November 1739, in Donald Burrows and Rosemary Dunhill, *Music and Theatre in Handel's World: The Family Papers of James Harris 1732–1780* (New York: Oxford University Press, 2002), 80, and in *Handel: Collected Documents*, iii, 537 (*pace* the commentary here, James Noel was not Gainsborough's son but his brother).
56 Shaftesbury to James Harris, 12 January 1744, in Burrows and Dunhill, *Music and Theatre*, 182–3, and *Handel: Collected Documents*, iv, 146–7. He could also have been the 'Hon. Mr. Noel' who subscribed to the first edition of Heighington's *Six Select Odes of Anacreon in Greek and Six of Horace in Latin* (London: John Simpson, [1745]).
57 Benjamin Martyn to Lord Shaftesbury, 1 August 1748, in Betty Matthews, 'Unpublished Letters concerning Handel', *Music & Letters*, 40 (1959), 266; *Handel: Collected Documents*, iv, 588, and Timms, 'Handel and *Comus* at Exton', 261.
58 Witness her opinion that *Susanna* was in 'the light operatical style' (letter to Elizabeth Harris, 11 February 1749, in Burrows and Dunhill, *Music and Theatre*, 254–5, and *Handel: Collected Documents*, iv, 634–5; original underline) and her reluctance to judge *Theodora* 'till I have heard it (at least) once more' (letter to Harris, 17–18 March 1750, in Burrows and Dunhill, *Music and Theatre*, 268–9, and *Handel: Collected Documents*, iv, 808–9).
59 Thomas Harris to James Harris, 26 April 1746, in Burrows and Dunhill, *Music and Theatre*, 226, and *Handel: Collected Documents*, iv, 405.
60 Burrows and Dunhill, *Music and Theatre*, 15–16; *Handel: Collected Documents*, iii, 145.
61 George Frideric Handel, *The Most Celebrated Songs in the Oratorio call'd Deborah* (London: I. Walsh, [1735]). The edition includes 'Choirs of angels', 'In

the battle fame pursuing', 'Tyrant now no more we dread thee', 'Endless flame thy days adorning', 'So much beauty sweetly blooming', 'To darkness eternal' and 'Joys in gentle trains appearing'.

62 See *Handel: Collected Documents*, iv, 460–61.
63 See below, p. 27 and Appendix II.10.
64 There was no prior notice of this performance: *Handel: Collected Documents*, iv, 657–8.
65 Martyn to Shaftesbury, 1 August 1748, cited in Matthews, 'Unpublished Letters', 267, and *Handel: Collected Documents*, iv, 588. See also Timms, 'Handel and *Comus* at Exton', 261–2.
66 *Lyric Repository: A Collection of Original, Ancient, & Modern Songs, Duets, Catches, Glees & Cantat: Selected for their Poetical and Literary Merit*, i (London: J. French, 1787), 65. The poem had already been published anonymously in *A Select Collection of Poems: With Notes Biographical and Historical*, iv (London: J. Nichols, 1780), 318.
67 'Thalestris arm's with spear and sheild [*sic*]': *A new Song The Words on a Lady of Quality Set by Mr Marchant Organest to the Duke of Rutland*. The other two songs are 'As Cupid one day roving saw', of which copies are preserved also in Cambridge (Fitzwilliam Museum) and Manchester (Chetham's Library), and 'In ancient Greece when Sappho sung'. A further song by Marchant, 'Cease, cease to argue, 'tis in vain', with 'the words by a nobleman', survives in Oxford (Harding Library).
68 'Servants wages Due for half a year at Michelmas 1713': Belvoir Castle archives (no pressmark).

2 Evidence from the Archives

Significant amounts of additional information on Gainsborough's intellectual and artistic interests and on cultural life at Exton Hall in the mid-eighteenth century are found in the twenty-one documents transcribed in Appendix II. The first seventeen of these documents are bills; the others are a manuscript book of poems (II.18), a substantial independent poem (II.19), a manuscript libretto of Handel's oratorio *Esther* (II.20) and the programme of what amounted to a small-scale music festival (II.21).

The bills were submitted by booksellers, stationers, binders, copyists, instrument repairers, a music teacher, a theatrical costumier, a scene-painter, carpenters and others, among whom three individuals stand out – Handel's copyist and manager Christopher Smith, the composer and violinist Michael Christian Festing and the sculptor Louis-François Roubiliac. The bills refer to goods and services supplied at various times over several years: one relates to the period 1743–46, the others to 1747–51. Nearly all of them were submitted after Gainsborough's death in March 1751 and receipted when paid by his executors or their agents: either he had failed to settle them punctually or the suppliers had failed to submit them when he had incurred the expenditure. The executors seem not to have noticed that a bill had occasionally been added up incorrectly, for they paid the claimants in full.

These documents contain a wealth of information on the price of goods and materials (e.g., paper, parchment, prints, printed books and music, bows and strings for instruments, busts by Roubiliac, hats, fabrics, whalebone and thread) and on the cost of labour (e.g., repairs to stringed instruments and harpsichords, harpsichord lessons, concert fees, music copying, music binding, porterage and carriage, carpentry and joinery, scene-building, scene-painting and costume-making). Much could be learnt from a comparison between these figures and those from other sources,[1] but attention is focused here on what the documents reveal about Gainsborough's artistic and intellectual interests and about cultural activity at Exton during his lifetime.

DOI: 10.4324/9781032627915-3

Books

The impression of Gainsborough's interests conveyed by Skynner's sermon and Browne's dedication is both confirmed and modified by the books that were bought by the earl during the last three years of his life. Evidence of his purchases is found in three of the bills – II.5 from John Cooke, the bookseller in Uppingham who published *Medicina Musica*; II.7 from Andrew Rogers, a 'stacioner' of Stamford (about eight miles from Exton), and II.10 from another stationer, William Shropshire. This last bill does not state where Shropshire was based, but since he charged for a wordbook of 'Solomon an Oratorio' on 17 March 1749, the day on which Handel's *Solomon* was first performed, his business must have been located in London. That this was indeed the case is corroborated by an announcement in the *Daily Advertiser* for 28 February 1776: 'On Monday [26 February] died at his son's house, in New Bond-street, Mr. William Shropshire, formerly an eminent bookseller in the same street. Aged 71'. Imprints reveal that he had been active as a bookseller and publisher from about 1730; a reference to 'Mess. Shropshire' in 1762 suggests that the business was then being run by at least two members of the family, presumably William and his son, but an imprint dated 1772 mentions only 'Walter' Shropshire, who appears then to have been in sole charge.[2]

Although Cooke was primarily a bookseller, he supplied a similar range of goods as the stationers Rogers and Shropshire and also, like Rogers, provided a binding service (see Table 2.1). It was Cooke, however, who met most of Gainsborough's requirements, including hats for male members of his family and staff.[3] Rogers sold Gainsborough more plays than Cooke or Shropshire, some of them in multiple copies, and also did more binding (the modest charge is deceptive). Shropshire did not supply paper and did very little binding: his bill relates almost entirely to books. The record of expenditure displayed in Table 2.1 seems therefore to show that it was mainly when Gainsborough was

Table 2.1 Lord Gainsborough's expenditure on books, etc., 1748–51.

Item \ Supplier	II.5 John Cooke 7 May 1748 to 17 March 1751	II.7 Andrew Rogers 7 April 1748 to 1 March 1751	II.10 William Shropshire 8 March 1749 to 10 February 1750
Binding	£ 8 8s. 0d.	£ 3 12s. 6d.	£ 4s. 0d.
Books	72 6 5	5 0	14 8 6
Music	4 9 6	1 6	3 0
Paper	21 7 0	15 0	
Prints	1 14 0	3 0	1 0
Sundry items	21 0 0		5 0
Totals	£ 129 4s. 11d.	£ 4 17s. 0d.	£ 15 1s. 6d.

in residence at Exton that he bought paper and had volumes bound, but that he purchased books both there and in London.

The three bills in question include over 220 entries for books and other printed material such as pamphlets and magazines. If Gainsborough had bought books at this rate since starting to subscribe to them in the mid-1720s (which he probably did not), his library would have numbered about 2,000 items by the time of his death in 1751. The entries in the bills vary in the amount of information they provide. Many give the name of an author or editor, some a short title, others a keyword. Some references specify the format (e.g., 8vo); others mention the number of volumes. In spite of the patchiness of this information, the vast majority of the publications in question can be identified with a high degree of confidence; for some entries two or three potential matches can be proposed, while in other cases the references are so brief or vague that it is impossible to pinpoint the work concerned. The results of this process are presented in the Index to Appendix II.

The number of books, in various subject areas, that Gainsborough purchased from 1748 to 1751 is shown in Table 2.2. The majority of his purchases fall under the heading 'Arts and Humanities'; the works listed under 'Sciences' form a comparatively small group, inflated perhaps by the treatment of Politics and Law as social sciences. Works on Chemistry and Physics are conspicuous by their absence, and Mathematics is represented merely by an instructional book on arithmetic.[4] Perhaps this imbalance explains why Skynner referred to Gainsborough's 'knowledge in' the principal arts but only his 'acquaintance with' history and the sciences – though the number of purchases in History implies a greater interest in this subject than is suggested by the word 'acquaintance'. There is no need to discuss every one of these purchases here, but a summary account of the works in each area, with a glance at some notable items, will enrich our knowledge of the earl and his outlook.

Table 2.2 Gainsborough's book purchases 1748–51, grouped by subject.

Arts and Humanities (157)		Sciences (34)	
Arts (104)	*Humanities (53)*	*Social sciences (16)*	*Natural sciences (18)*
Literature – Classical 13	History – Ancient 12	Law 6	Geography 4
Literature – Modern 71	History – Modern 18	Politics 8	Medicine 6
Other arts 9	Philosophy 4	Reference 2	Natural world 8
Criticism 5	Religion* 19		
Reference 6			

* Not including unspecified Bibles, Testaments, Prayer Books, etc.

His purchases relating to Geography suggest that his interests extended beyond the shores of Great Britain. These acquisitions include a 'complete system' of the subject (by Bowen), illustrated with seventy maps, reports on the discovery of Madeira (by Alcoforado) and travels in South America (by La Condamine), and an anonymous account of George Anson's 'voyage to the South Seas' – i.e., his circumnavigation of the globe in 1740–44.[5] The purchases on Nature, too, include a general survey of the subject (Pluche, translated by Samuel Humphreys), illustrated with copper plates; Humphreys is known to Handelians as the author of the 'additional words' in the 1732 version of his oratorio *Esther*, as the librettist of his *Deborah* and *Athalia* and as the translator of his operas *Poro*, *Rinaldo* (1731), *Ezio*, *Sosarme* and *Orlando*.[6] There are also a number of more specialised works on the natural world – Edwards on birds (also with copper plates) and Gilpin, Miller and Whitmill on gardens and gardening. A love of country sports is suggested by books on fishing (including Walton's *Compleat Angler*) and the anonymous *Thoughts on* [...] *Game Law*. Curiosity about the human body is demonstrated by purchases on Medicine, including studies of anatomy (Albinus, Hartley), afflictions (Lobb and anonymous), and the effects on human beings of air (Arbuthnot) and tea (Short) – all published in or after 1730: perhaps Gainsborough's interest in these subjects had been stimulated by Browne's *Medicina Musica* (1729).

His purchases on Religion, even excluding Bibles, Testaments and liturgical books, outnumber those on any subject other than modern Literature. They range from biographies of Jesus Christ (Du Pin) and St Paul (Annet), via collections of sermons by Atterbury, Littleton, Seed and Yardley, to studies of prophecy and the Resurrection (both by Sherlock) and to a discussion of the Church of England (Jones), of which Gainsborough was a member. Given his apparently strong interest in religion, it is surprising to find that Philosophy is represented only by a 'compendious system' (Rowning), a philosophy of musical sounds (Smith) and the maxims of La Rochefoucauld. Among the publications on Politics, most of which are anonymous, the most prominent work is Bolingbroke's *Letters on the Spirit of Patriotism*. One of the anonymous items discusses the resignation of Lord Chesterfield in 1748 as Secretary of State for the Northern Department; others are concerned with British interests in relation to, for example, Gibraltar and the Northern Powers. Pride of place among works on Law goes to Montesquieu's *Spirit of Laws*, which Gainsborough purchased both in the original French and in English translation. Military matters are considered in writings both on Law (Anon., *The Antient and Present State of Military Law*) and on Politics (Muller).

As suggested above, Gainsborough appears to have had a particular interest in History. His purchases on ancient history include the maps designed by Jean-Baptiste Bourguignon d'Anville to illustrate Charles Rollin's study of the Egyptians, Carthaginians, Assyrians and others. He also bought works on ancient Greece (Stanyan and Venuti) and Rome (Florus, Herodian and

Pomey), Nepos's *Lives of Illustrious Men* and an anonymous *Life of Augustus Cæsar*. Apart from ancient history, Gainsborough purchased general surveys by Sale and Salmon, and books on Genoa (Oudart Feudrix) and the conquest of Mexico (Ribadeneyra), but he spent most liberally on works about England – Guthrie's *General History*, Holinshed's *Chronicles*, Godwin's commentary on English bishops and cardinals, Savile's biography of King Charles II and Pote's *History* [...] *of Windsor Castle, and the* [...] *Chapel of St. George*, historic buildings that he would have known as a schoolboy at nearby Eton College.

Pote's Greek grammar (*Græcæ grammaticæ rudimenta*) and Aler's Latin thesaurus (*Gradus ad Parnassum*) are prominent among Gainsborough's purchases relating to classical Literature. As examples of the Greek classics he opted for Æsop's *Fables*, Homer's *Odyssey* and Pindar's *Odes* – all in translation[7] – while for Latin he purchased Cæsar and Horace in the original, Cicero and Ovid in translation, and an edition of Virgil's *Georgics* in Latin and English. He also bought studies of mythology by Banier and Blackwell.

To judge by the number of items that he purchased, modern Literature is the subject in which Gainsborough was most interested. The majority of his English acquisitions consist of novels, plays and poetry, but he also bought letters and memoirs by, for example, Pope and Laetitia Pilkington, respectively. His taste in novels was broad, ranging from Defoe's somewhat autobiographical and didactic *Robinson Crusoe* and Richardson's epistolary *Clarissa* to Fielding's comic *History of Tom Jones, a Foundling* and Cleland's erotic *Memoirs of a Woman of Pleasure* (Fanny Hill). In addition to individual plays, which are dealt with separately below, Gainsborough also bought collected editions of the dramatic works of Congreve, Dryden, Shakespeare and Steele. Poetry is represented by a number of English authors, including Hughes, Pope and Thomson,[8] and by one of the several available translations of Tasso's *Gerusalemme liberata*.

Gainsborough's interest in arts other than literature is not strongly reflected in the books that he bought between 1748 and 1751. Apart from Robert Smith's *Harmonics, or the Philosophy of Musical Sounds*, referred to above, the only music book that he purchased is one of the two by Thomas Salmon that had been published in 1672 and 1688, respectively. On the subject of the visual arts Gainsborough bought Aglionby's *Choice Observations on* [...] *Painting* (which includes an edition of Vasari's *Lives of the Most Eminent Painters*), Pozzo's *Rules and Examples of Perspective*, Gwynn's *Essay on Design* and an instructional book on drawing (Lens). His love of theatre is demonstrated by biographical accounts of Thomas Betterton and Colley Cibber ('with an historical view of the Stage') and by John Hill's *The Actor: A Treatise on the Art of Playing* (1750 – two years after Gainsborough's participation in *Comus*). Artistic criticism is represented by two works on Shakespeare (Edwards and [Holt]), two on poetry, painting and music (Aglionby and Dubos) and Lancaster's *Plan of an Essay on*

Delicacy. The list of his acquisitions is completed by a number of dictionaries (Classical, English and Italian), a French grammar, a French vocabulary, an Italian primer, a companion for travellers in England, and a *Universal Pocket-Book* containing a map of the world and information on a range of practical subjects relating to life in England and Scotland.

Gainsborough's acquisitions include a remarkable number of works by French authors. In the case of La Condamine, La Morlière and Pascal, he bought only the original French version, but he purchased both the French original and the English translation of Montesquieu's *Esprit des lois* (as noted above) and, conversely, both the French translation and the English original of Sherlock's *Use and Intent of Prophecy*. His edition of Molière contained the plays in both French and English, and at least eleven of his purchases were translations from French – the anonymous *Life of Augustus Cæsar* and the works by Banier, De Curli, Dubos, Du Pin, [Grafigny], Jolyot (*The Sopha*), La Rochefoucauld, Lesage, Oudart Feudrix and Pluche. This emphasis on French presumably reflects the importance of the language in the eighteenth century both as the medium of international diplomacy and polite European society and, as a consequence, in the education of young men and women.[9]

Gainsborough's purchases also include a considerable number of works that were published with an expressly educational purpose. The words 'for schools' or 'for the use of schools' appear on the title page of the anonymous book on arithmetic, mentioned above, and of the works on ancient history by Florus, [Lockman] and Pomey (*An Abridgment*). Pote's Greek grammar and Aler's Latin thesaurus were originally intended for use by young people ('in usum [studiosæ] juventutis'); Gwynn's *Essay on Design* included proposals for 'a public academy [...] for educating the British youth in drawing'; Lens's drawing book was aimed at 'young gentlemen and ladies'; Keach's book of religious instruction was subtitled a 'child's and youth's delight', and Humphreys' translation of Pluche's *Spectacle de la nature* was intended 'to excite the curiosity and form the minds of youth'. In 1729, the year after her marriage, the Countess of Gainsborough was the dedicatee of William Hatchett's translation of the Marchioness de Lambert's *Advice from a Mother to her Son and Daughter*, and in 1731 the countess subscribed to a Dublin edition of the same work (*A New-Year's-Gift, being Advice from a Mother* [...]). Gainsborough himself subscribed to the marchioness's *Letters to her Son and Daughter on True Education &c. &c. &c.* in 1749. That the earl and the countess acquired all these items suggests not only that they were interested in the education of young people but that they regarded education as important and took steps to encourage and enrich the development of their children.[10]

In short, Gainsborough's purchases reveal a considerable amount about his interests and character. Although it cannot be assumed that he dipped into all his acquisitions, let alone read them from cover to cover, or that he was equally interested in all the topics that they treat, he must have been an intelligent individual with an interest in most of the subjects concerned – the world as a whole, human society and history, national and international politics and law, religion, languages, literature and other arts. Assuming this to be so, he must also have been – or have become – a well-educated gentleman who identified with the political, social and cultural contexts represented by this literary culture. Furthermore, his books were not meant for him alone. In the family portrait mentioned above,[11] he is depicted with his wife and three of their daughters and also, in his right hand, with an open book of which facing pages are displayed to the viewer. The message is clear. The owner of the house may have had a private study, but by the mid-eighteenth century the library, with books and magazines for pleasure as well as edification, was intended for the whole family, their friends and their guests, and was increasingly being used as a living room.[12]

Ultimately, Gainsborough's acquisition of printed materials also reflects the enormous increase during the century in the publication and distribution, throughout the British Isles, of literary items ranging from broadsheets to multi-volume works, on an ever-expanding variety of subjects. The growth in the availability of printed materials enabled the population, over time, to become better informed and better equipped to exercise judgement and cultivate taste. By the end of the century it was possible 'to imagine, to hold and even to own the works of literature and art, or at least copies of them, which had been enshrined by London critics, commercial booksellers and art dealers as Britain's cultural heritage'.[13]

Music

Two-thirds of the documents in Appendix II are concerned in whole or in part with matters relating to music. The topics most frequently mentioned are the purchase of music and paper, the binding and copying of music, and the maintenance of musical instruments. One bill (II.1), however, refers to the eighteen days in 1748–9 that a carpenter named Kell (or Kellem) Berrey spent working 'att the Musick Rooms'. No music rooms are listed in the inventory of Exton Hall compiled in 1717, so these must have been a creation of the 4th Earl – a powerful statement of his intention to cultivate an art that clearly was one of his principal interests. When the rooms were created is not known, and Berrey's bill sheds no light on the question: it is not clear whether he improved existing music facilities or converted existing rooms for musical purposes. All that can be said for certain is that by Michaelmas 1748, when he started work, Exton could boast one or more music rooms that were undergoing renovation or construction. Interestingly, the late 1740s is the period when Charles Jennens also created his music room at Gopsall Hall, about forty-five miles west of Exton: he had inherited the Hall in 1747, and his (unfinished) music room was described by the engineer John Grundy in 1750.[14] Whether Jennens was influenced by Gainsborough or vice versa – or whether either was influenced by the Holywell Music Room in Oxford, which opened in

1748 – is impossible to tell. It does seem, however, that music rooms were in fashion at that time.

Instruments

Four of the bills are concerned with the maintenance of musical instruments – three of them with stringed instruments. On 23 November 1743, the earliest date in any of the documents in Appendix II, a Stamford cabinet-maker named William Lowe charged 5s. 0d. for repairing and varnishing a violin and a violoncello (II.3). In an age when workmen specialised in particular skills,[15] it may have been unusual for such instruments to be entrusted to a cabinet-maker: presumably there was no specialist in the vicinity of Exton, and Lowe had acquired sufficient expertise and experience to undertake repairs. The second of these bills (II.13) was submitted by Festing, whom Gainsborough and his wife had supported by subscribing to three publications of his music (1730, 1731 and 1747). Between November 1747 and January 1748 Festing supplied strings, bridges and pins for a violin, and bows for a violin and two violoncellos; he also paid for the 'twisting of handles with catlings' – presumably the winding of catling strings round the handle of a bow to improve or enlarge the grip. Finally, between September 1748 and May 1749 Alice Walmsly supplied strings for a violin, one or two violas, one or two violoncellos, a double bass and 'a little base'; she also sold two bows – one with a screw, the other without – and repaired a double bass (II.12). It is possible that Mrs Walmsly was related to Peter Wamsley, a London-based maker of stringed instruments who was active in *c.* 1725–45;[16] maybe she carried on the business after he had died. If so, she presumably supplied her goods and services to Gainsborough and his family when they were in town. All three bills confirm the impression, given by his subscriptions, that the earl encouraged the performance of music for strings, possibly in London as well as at Exton. The documents do not enable us to estimate the size of the Exton ensemble, but if two double basses were needed for an acceptable balance to be achieved, the band may have been quite large. This possibility is supported by Benjamin Martyn's description of the orchestra for the performances of *Comus* in 1748 as 'full'[17] and by anonymous references to concerts by 'the whole Band' in 1750 (II.21).

Festing's bill prompts further speculation. As a virtuoso violinist and composer, Festing was one of the most prominent musicians in London during the second quarter of the eighteenth century; in 1738 he was one of the three founder-members of the Fund for the Support of Decay'd Musicians and their Families (now the Royal Society of Musicians of Great Britain). His bill is the only known piece of evidence that he also serviced violins. It is not clear whether he ran a separate business as a dealer in stringed instruments and their accessories or provided this service as an adjunct to teaching, as Felice Giardini appears to have done.[18] Taken together with the subscriptions to his works, the bill suggests that Gainsborough and his family not only were acquainted with Festing but also may have engaged him as a teacher. If they first met in the 1720s or 1730s, their acquaintance could well have continued after 1742, when Festing began a ten-year stint as the first director of music at Ranelagh Gardens. Gainsborough's cousin John Manners, 3rd Duke of Rutland, had established a precedent for this kind of arrangement in the 1720s by employing the violinist Giovanni Stefano Carbonelli while he was also leader of the orchestra at the Drury Lane theatre:[19] Carbonelli must have spent part of the year at the Manners family seat, Belvoir Castle, fifteen miles (as the crow flies) north of Exton, while continuing to pursue his career as a performer in London.[20] Only further research can reveal whether Festing, too, divided his time in this way.

The fourth bill concerned with the maintenance of instruments was submitted by George Wright, who is described on the outside of the document (II.6) as 'Musick Master'. In this bill he claims reimbursement and payment for 'Strings and Repairs for ye Harpsicords', of which there must have been at least two at Exton Hall.

Purchase of Music

Purchases of music are documented in three bills, including those from John Cooke and Andrew Rogers, already discussed. The entries in the bills do not actually specify purchase but can be distinguished with confidence from those for binding.[21] It is interesting to note – though possibly coincidental – that Gainsborough made the earliest of his purchases in the year after he stopped acquiring music by subscription. Cooke's bill (II.5) contains the largest number of music entries, and they extend over the longest period of time, from 7 May 1748 to 5 February 1751. With the exception of Corelli's violin sonatas, op. 5, all the music supplied by Cooke was vocal. It seems, nevertheless, to have been varied in character, including part of Croft's *Musica Sacra*, Boyce's pastoral entertainment *The Chaplet*, and collections of shorter pieces – anthems, psalm tunes and hymns (*Voice of Melody*), amusing secular songs (*Antidote against Melancholy*; *The Merry Man's Companion*), English and Scottish folk songs (*Orpheus*) and 'songs' from the Italian pasticcio *Orazio*.

The bill from Andrew Rogers (II.7) records only one purchase of music – the 'Comic Tunes in Queen Mab', on 1 March 1751. The title page of this publication begins as follows:[22]

> The Comic Tunes in Queen Mab. As they are perform'd at the Theatre Royal Drury Lane. Set for the Violin, German Flute or Hoboy, with a Thorough Bass for the Harpsicord; Composed by the Society of the Temple of Apollo publish'd by authority. London printed for J. Oswald and sold at his Musick Shop in St. Martin's Church Yard. [...]

The pantomime *Queen Mab*, by the actor Henry Woodward, had been presented by David Garrick on 26 December 1750; with the author in a starring role, it proved exceedingly popular, receiving forty-five performances in its first season.[23] The tunes must have been printed early in 1751. The publisher, James Oswald (1710–69), was a Scottish cellist, composer and publisher who had moved to London in 1741 and been granted a royal licence six years later to print his own compositions.[24] In 1748 he was credited by the poet James Thomson with the invention of the Aeolian harp; having mentioned the instrument in his poem *The Castle of Indolence*, of which Gainsborough was billed for a copy on 14 May (see II.5), Thomson referred to Oswald as its inventor in a footnote to his *Ode on Æolus's Harp*.[25]

The Society of the Temple of Apollo, not to be confused with Maurice Greene's Apollo Academy, must have been founded in or soon after 1747, probably by Oswald and possibly in collaboration with others.[26] It is mentioned in at least fourteen editions of music published by Oswald between then and 1762:

The Temple of Apollo, or The Theatre of the Muses for the month of April 1747 [...]. *Corrected & approv'd by the Society of the Temple of Apollo*

Six Songs compos'd for the Temple of Apollo. To which is added A Favourite Cantata ['The Despairing Shepherd', words by John Gay] *set to Musick by M^r. Chas Burney.* Opera II. Libr. 1 [*c.* 1747]

Sammartini, Giuseppe, *Six Sonatas or Duets for two German Flutes. Compos'd for the Temple of Apollo* [...]. Opera prima. Book 1^a [*c.* 1750]

Apollo's Collection, being XII Duettos for two German Flutes or two Violins composed by [...] *Geminiani* [...] *Martini* [...] *Jommelli* [...] *Rameau* [...] *Blavet* [...] *Oswald*, Lib. 1mo. *Corrected and approv'd of, by the Society* [*c.* 1750]

The Music in the Masque of Alfred [...] *As it is perform'd at the Theatre Royal* [...] *Compos'd by the Society of the Temple of Apollo* [1751]

The Comic Tunes in Queen Mab [...]. [1751]

The Songs in Queen Mab. As they are perform'd at the Theatre Royal in Drury Lane; Compos'd by the Society of the Temple of Apollo: Sung by M.^{r} [but the last song by 'Master'] *Vernon* [1751]

Apollo's Collection, being Six Sonatas or Duets for two German Flutes or two Violins by [...] *Tartini* [...] *Jommelli* [...] *Martini* [...] *Rameau* [...] *Blavet* [...] *Oswald*, Book 2^d [1752]

A Collection of Songs as they are perform'd at the Publick Gardens [...] *Corrected & approv'd, by the Society of the Temple of Apollo*, Opera 2^d, Book 2^d [*c.* 1752]

A Collection of Songs sung at the Publick Gardens [...] *Compos'd for the Society of the Temple of Apollo*, Opera 2da, Book 3^d [*c.* 1752]

The Comic Tunes in Queen Mab [...] *Compos'd by the Society of the Temple of Apollo* [*c.* 1755]

Dothel Figlio [pseudonym for James Oswald], *Six Sonatas for two Violins or German Flutes* [...] Op. 3.[za] *Corrected and approv'd of, by the Society of the Temple of Apollo* [c. 1755]
[Reid, John], *Six Solos for a German Flute or Violin* [...] *by I. R. Esqr. A Member of the Temple of Apollo* [1756]
[Reid], *A Second Sett of Six Solos for a German Flute or Violin* [...] *by I. R. Esqr. A Member of the Temple of Apollo* [1762].

The meetings and concerts of the society were held at a house in Queen Square, and the membership appears to have included Charles Burney, John Reid and Giuseppe Sammartini. In her memoirs of Burney (1832) his daughter Fanny claimed that her father composed 'the whole of the music' in *Queen Mab*,[27] but a reprint of the *Comic Tunes*, published in 1769 by William Randall and Messrs Straight and Skillern, names Oswald as the composer. It is possible that both Burney and Oswald contributed to the score and that Gainsborough purchased a copy because he or a member of his family had attended and enjoyed a performance of the pantomime.

The third bill recording purchases of music is of particular interest because it was submitted by Christopher Smith, described here as 'Mr Handels wrighter' (II.11).[28] Like the bills from Festing and Shropshire, it demonstrates that Gainsborough, as well as drawing on resources close to Exton, cultivated relations with the musical world in London; furthermore, it also shows that, having welcomed Handel to his country seat in 1745, he remained in touch with the composer's senior assistant, at least. While Festing looked after stringed instruments and Shropshire dealt mainly in books, Smith provided music, in this case mostly printed. The '60 printed ouvertures' that he supplied on 3 January 1750 are listed anonymously but were undoubtedly by Handel. In October 1749 Walsh had advertised the publication of the 'Tenth Collection' of six Handel overtures, along with the following note: '*N.B.* This Sett with 54 already published, complete the Overtures from all Mr. Handel's Operas and Oratorios'.[29] Gainsborough evidently bought them all and had them bound by Benjamin Christian (II.4), who on 30 March 1750 charged him 18s. 9d. for binding 'Handel's Overtures 15 Vol^s at 1^s–3^d each'. These overtures are the only musical works for which the documents provide evidence of both purchase and binding. Smith also supplied Gainsborough with Handel's 'new' concertos (presumably his *Twelve Grand Concertos*, op. 6), his 'old' ones (presumably his *Concerti Grossi*, op. 3), 'Corelli's D.^{o}' (*Concerti Grossi*, op. 6), '12 printed Books of Sampson' (wordbooks) and 'part of a Chorus in Sampson', presumably in manuscript. On 22 September 1750 Smith claimed reimbursement for 'the Carrige of the Oratorio of Sampson', an entry suggesting that he and his assistants in London prepared the manuscript copy of Handel's *Samson* that had been bound in three volumes by Rogers, who had charged Gainsborough 12s. 0d. for the job on 22 August. Smith's bill also includes five books of opera dances (presumably the five books of *Comic*

Tunes to [...] *Opera Dances* published by Walsh in 1741–7), a song in 'Demetrius' (the London 1737 version of Pescetti's *Demetrio*) and four more songs, apparently from the same opera.

Binding

Rogers' bill for the binding of *Samson* shows that Gainsborough possessed music by Handel for which the documents offer no evidence of purchase. This is not the only example. On 15 April, 28 April and 8 May 1748 Rogers charged Gainsborough 3s. 0d. for binding each of the three parts of Handel's *Joshua*, which had received its first performance on 9 March. Rogers' charges must refer to a manuscript copy of the score, not a printed edition, and the gaps between his dates suggest that each part of the oratorio was bound as soon as it had been copied. On 11 April Rogers had also billed Gainsborough for 'a Broad Folio 6 Quires fools. Cap. Rul'd'; even if the word 'rul'd' referred to staves, this would not have been enough paper for the entire oratorio, though it could have supplemented an existing stock of paper at Exton Hall. Be that as it may, it appears that Gainsborough ordered a manuscript copy of *Joshua* and had it bound within two months of the work's first performance – fast work! He also possessed a Royal folio copy of *Israel in Egypt*, for the binding of which Rogers charged the surprisingly low sum of 7s. 6d. on 8 July 1748; the purchase of '30 Q.^{r} paper' for which Cooke had charged 19s. 6d. on 1 July could conceivably relate to this oratorio, though one would have expected the bill to specify the size of the paper. On 28 December 1749 Cooke himself charged the seemingly large sum of 6s. 0d. for binding one volume of unspecified 'songs' by Handel and another containing some of Hasse's *Venetian Ballads*.

The bills submitted by Rogers, Cooke and Benjamin Christian also include charges for binding unspecified pieces of music that cannot now be identified. Rogers billed Gainsborough on 12 August 1748 for half-binding 'a Quire of Royal 4.to Musick' (2s. 0d.) and on 2 September for '4 Vol.^{s} of Royal 4.to Musick' (8s. 0d.). In 1749 he charged 1s. 8d. for 'a Quarto Volume of Manuscript Musick.— (not Letter'd)' on 3 March, and 16s. 6d. for '11 Musick Books Royal 4.to of different Sizes (as to thickness &c.^{a})' – an average of 1s. 6d. per book – on 7 April. The varying thickness of these books suggests that they may have been a set of parts for performance. In addition to the songs by Handel and Hasse, mentioned above, and around the same time (28 December 1749), Cooke also bound '7. Folio Vols musick Double=b^d silk & Double Lrd [Lettered]' at a cost of £2 12s. 0d. – nearly 7s. 6d. per volume. The luxurious quality and exceptionally high cost of this binding suggest that these volumes held particular significance for Gainsborough or his family or perhaps were intended as a gift. There is no way of knowing whether the volumes contained scores or separate parts, one volume per instrument in an ensemble. Although it is very unlikely that parts intended for use in performance would have been given such a handsome or expensive form of binding, the number of volumes happens to reflect the fact that *concerti grossi* were normally published in seven parts. Handel's concertos op. 3 and op. 6 can be ruled out, however, because Cooke's invoice for binding these volumes anticipates by nearly eight months the date (11 August 1750) on which Smith charged Gainsborough for their purchase. The only set of concertos that is named in the documents and appears to fit the bill is John Hebden's op. 2 [*c.* 1745], to which the 4th Earl subscribed, but there is no obvious reason why these works should have been singled out for such special treatment.

Paper and Copying

Given that one of the volumes of unidentified music, mentioned above, was a manuscript, it seems likely that other unspecified pieces presented for binding also were in handwritten form. This possibility is strengthened by bills for the purchase of paper and the copying of music. The only entry in the documents that refers explicitly to music paper is Cooke's 'Royall Paper for musick' (28 December 1749), but since Alice Walmsly ran a business concerned with stringed instruments, it is probable that the '2 Quire of Royal paper' and 'two Royal Books' (II.12) that she sold to Gainsborough in December 1748 and March 1749 were intended for music. There are two references in the documents to paper described as ruled, of which the earlier was discussed in connection with *Joshua*. The later entry, 'Folio Paper book ruld' (II.5: 3 July 1750), is more problematic. A book ruled with staves would have been an unusual vehicle for a substantial musical work such as an oratorio, for which unbound quires were more practical, but it could have served as an album for shorter pieces or for teaching materials. It could conceivably be related, therefore, to the fact that from 21 July to the third week of October Gainsborough's daughters received harpsichord lessons from the music master, George Wright (II.6) – although a folio volume might not have sat well on the instrument's music stand. Failing that, it is also possible that the book contained no staves at all but had been ruled for a non-musical purpose, perhaps as a ledger for the keeping of accounts.

Between April 1748 and March 1751, in addition to these modest quantities of Royal and ruled papers, Gainsborough also bought large amounts of paper of other kinds. From Cooke (II.5) he purchased 'paper' (*tout court*) – 340 quires, and five consignments of an unspecified size; some of this paper was accompanied by wax, suggesting that it was to be used for correspondence. Cooke also supplied him with ten quires of 'best Dutch fools Cap' and ten of 'best cut Dutch paper', thirty-five quires of Demy (ten quarto, three folio and the rest unspecified), seven 'Broad Folio paper books', two quires of 'gold imbost paper', three batches of gilt paper, two lots of pasteboard and '1 Skin of Parchm^t to Mr Chapman'. Seven and a half quires of cartridge paper, presumably for drawing or painting but possibly for music, and six sheets of embossed paper were purchased from Rogers (II.7).

To judge from the documents, only a small proportion of this paper was used for the copying of music: music-copying is the subject of only four brief entries in the bills, and all of these date from 1750. Two of them relate to unspecified anthems, the others to parts of Handel's *Samson*. For two batches of anthems, copied on 31 July and 6 August, Christian charged a total of 12s. 1½d. (II.4); by specifying the number of pages in each batch – fifty-seven and forty, respectively – he made clear that his charge was 1½d. per page. This information is useful, for on 6 July he had charged 2s. 4½d. for 'Writing a Vocal part in sampson for L:^{d} Campden'. Lord Campden was Gainsborough's ten-year-old son, Baptist Noel, who had appeared as 'a little Bacchanal' in the revival of *Comus* in 1748. If Christian charged 1½d. per page for copying the boy's part in *Samson*, the part must have consisted of nineteen pages of music; what exactly it contained is unknown, but it presumably was used by Lord Campden in the performance of the oratorio at Exton in August–September 1750 (II.21). *Samson* is mentioned again in the bill from Christopher Smith, who on 22 September charged 2s. 6d. for 'part of a Chorus in Sampson' (II.11). This is a tantalising reference, because the nature of the 'part' is unclear and Gainsborough's score of the work had been bound a full month before Smith's billing date. The most likely explanation is that the 'part' was copied before the performance and Smith was a little behind with his billing. The final entry for copying is dated 10 December, when Christian charged 1s. 6d. for further 'Anthems Writing' – a job that amounted to only twelve pages.

Performance

If we assume that most of the music mentioned above – whether copied, purchased or acquired by subscription – was intended for performance or private practice at Exton, it is surprising to find that musical performance is mentioned in only three of the documents. One of these (II.9) comprises two bills – one for bell-ringing, and the other for 'Concert playing' on 4 and 7 February 1751. The latter identifies the concert players as Francis, Michael and John Sharp, but not the instruments or the music they played. It is tempting to assume that these musicians were related to the remarkable Sharp family who held music parties on the Thames from 1753 and were depicted by Johan Zoffany in a celebrated group portrait dating from 1779–80, but the members of this large family spent their lives mainly in Durham, Northumberland, London and Wicken Park (Northamptonshire) and are not known from other sources to have broken their journeys at Exton.[30]

The other two documents relate to the summer of 1750. George Wright's bill (II.6) reveals not only that he replaced harpsichord strings and repaired the instruments, of which, clearly, the family possessed more than one, but that from July to October he gave harpsichord lessons to two of Gainsborough's daughters – presumably Jane (aged 17) and Juliana (15). The third document (II.21) is an anonymous account of a visit to Exton, written on a tiny chit of paper, possibly an entry torn out of a diary. This is the source of the information about the 'week-long programme of musical events', mentioned by Gerard Noel,[31] which included the following performances:

1750
Tuesday 28 August
    evening: music in the park 'in three different trees' and a concert 'by the whole Band'
Wednesday 29 August
    morning: concert after breakfast
    evening: *Alexander's Feast*
Thursday 30 August
    evening: *Samson*
Friday 31 August
    morning: *Samson* 'again'
    evening: concert of music 'of the whole Band'
Saturday 1 September
    morning: *Samson* 'again'
    evening: concert of music
Sunday 2 September
    anthem for the funeral of Queen Caroline (*The Ways of Zion do mourn*) and 'othere proper Musick in the Chapel'

The description of the music on 28 August is not entirely clear, but it presumably means that, out in the park, music was played in amongst three groups of trees. Outdoor music had become increasingly popular among a wide variety of people through the influence of London's pleasure gardens and especially after the opening of the refurbished Vauxhall Gardens in 1732;[32] at Exton, *Comus* had been intended for performance in the garden in 1745 and been staged there in 1748. It is not known what music was played among the trees in 1750, but presumably it was instrumental. The concerts given by 'the whole band' may have featured the concertos and overtures by Corelli and Handel, mentioned in II.4 (30 March 1750) and II.11 (3 January and 11 August 1750), while those by unspecified forces could have included solo sonatas by Corelli and Festing, and songs and dances from contemporary operas (II.5, 2 January and 28 December 1749, and II.11, 11 August 1750); maybe Gainsborough's daughters played the harpsichord in some of these works. The performance of *Alexander's Feast* was presumably related to the fact that the countess had subscribed to the publication of the full score of the work (1738).

As already seen, *Samson* looms large in the documents. Gainsborough had been charged in July 1750 for a vocal part for his son (II.4) and in August for a dozen wordbooks (II.11) and the binding of the score (II.7); in September Christopher Smith was to bill him for part of a chorus and for carriage of the score (II.11), presumably from London to Exton. The prominence of this oratorio in the records may be due to the fact that the work is based on Milton, but it also strengthens the possibility that James Noel had been instrumental in persuading Handel to compose it. All the same, the idea that *Samson* was performed complete on three consecutive days is hardly credible: one act per day seems a more likely schedule. Before the evening concerts on the Friday and Saturday the gentlemen played bowls, evidently a favourite pastime at Exton (II.19). The works performed in the chapel on Sunday, among them *The Ways of Zion Do Mourn*, could have been among the anthems copied by Christian in the summer of 1750 (II.4, 31 July), though the programme could also have included items from Croft's *Musica Sacra* (II.5).

There are, nevertheless, some notable discrepancies between the information provided by the documents and the performances at Exton that are known to have taken place. Gainsborough paid for scores of *Joshua* and *Israel in Egypt* to be bound (II.7, 15 and 28 April, 8 May and 8 July 1748) and bought printed wordbooks of *Solomon* and *Messiah* (II.10), but there is no indication – other than the reference to 'Oratorios' in Mrs Smith's letter of 31 August 1748 – that any of these works was performed. More striking, perhaps, is the absence from the documents of any mention of *Comus* or *Deborah*, both of which, according to Benjamin Martyn's letter of 1 August 1748 to Lord Shaftesbury, were performed at Exton that summer. Furthermore, of the seven works by Handel from which movements were selected for inclusion in *Comus*,[33] only *Samson* and *Esther* are represented in the documents – the latter by only a manuscript libretto that cannot date from before late August 1747 (II.20). Movements from Handel's *Alcina*, *L'Allegro*, *Belshazzar*, *Deborah* and *Flavio* – and also, apparently, from Arne's *Comus* – must have been available in some form at Exton, but none of these works is mentioned in the documents.

Theatre

Stages and Scenery

Although the title 'Comus' is not found in the 'theatrical' documents in Appendix II, the 1748 production of the work is clearly the subject of the earliest of these bills. Three years earlier, as James Noel wrote to Lord Shaftesbury, the masque was 'intended to have been perform'd in the Garden, but the weather would not favour that Design. We contriv'd however to entertain the Company there afterwards with an Imitation of Vaux Hall'.[34] In 1748, as Martyn explained in his letter of 1 August, it was performed in a garden theatre, specially constructed for the occasion:

> Last Friday Evening, a little before Sunset, We were all summon'd to a Grove in the Garden, which for a fortnight before had been forbidden Ground to Lady Bath, Mrs Noel and myself. After a little winding walk in it, we found our Selves in the midst of a Theatre, at one end of which was a Box with four Rows of Benches, rais'd above one another, and 20 feet in front. The Intermediate space between that and the Stage was bounded on the Sides by high Trees [...] When Comus bad the Revels begin, the Back Scene was drawn up, and behind it was another space (of the same Bigness as that where the Box and Theatre were) with a high Tree in the Middle, and surrounded by high ones, which were fill'd with Lights in the most agreeable Manner; so that the Stage fill'd with Actors, who lin'd the side Scenes; (which are prettily painted) a Row of Lemon Trees with large fruit tied on the Boughs, just behind the Stage, and the Illuminated Grove beyond it, made the most Romantick Fairy Scene imaginable.[35]

Since 1 August 1748 was a Monday, the performance 'last Friday' must have taken place on 29 July; the venue, 'a Grove in the Garden', had been out of bounds for a 'fortnight' (which may be a rough approximation). Martyn's testimony is corroborated by a bill from the carpenter John Fancort (II.15[a]1), who began 'Setting up scens in the Gardin' on 13 July and spent a total of '17 days' on this and on 'taking [them and, presumably, the theatre] down' when they were no longer needed. It is probable that the majority of these days were spent on setting up and that some were left clear for rehearsal before the performance. Fancort was assisted by a team of seven men, working various numbers of days; six of them earned 1s. per day,[36] but Will Fancort, presumably John's son and an apprentice, was paid at half that rate. The work of building and striking the theatre and scenery took a total of ninety-five 'man-days' and cost £4 9s. 0d.

Further bills for the construction of stages were submitted by John Fancort on behalf of himself and his assistants. His bill of 12 March 1750 (II.15[b]) mentions three days spent on the setting up and taking down of a stage in the chapel; by then his rate had increased to 1s. 6d. per day, and Will Fancort's to 1s. The same bill cites, in addition, thirty days for the 'making of a new Stage and Setting up'. This was presumably the stage that is mentioned both in a bill from Phillip Gann (II.16), also dating from 1750 and for thirty days' work, and in an undated bill from Anthony Herring (II.8) claiming, for himself, '25 Days Works helping to Build the Stage in the Hall' and, for his apprentice, twenty days' work. It is possible, also, that John Newbould's bill of 17 November 1750 for 'Covering the sound board' (II.17[b]) refers to this stage. On 7 June 1751 Samuel Goodwin submitted a retrospective bill 'For

Painting the New Stage for his Lordship's Account' and for 'The Model of the Stage' (II.2), but it is not known when this work was done.

John Fancort and others also submitted bills for the construction, erection and repair of scenery. As well as building the stage and scenery in the garden in July 1748, he and Will Fancort, John Hobs and Kell Berrey, presumably that summer, put up scenes in the Hall: the first time they did so the job took four days (II.15[a]2), but on the last occasion it included 'making other new things about them [the scenes]' and lasted sixteen days (II.15[a]3). Many of the bills submitted by carpenters cover long periods of work, rather than precise dates: between Michaelmas 1748 and Michaelmas 1749 both Berrey and his 'man' spent two days setting up scenes and two more taking them down (II.1); between September 1749 and December 1750 John Fancort worked for '33 Days Setting up Senes [sic] in ye hall and Repairing of Them' and '92 Days making of frames for ye Senes and other work a bout them' (II.15[b]); between 18 March 1750 and an unspecified date in December Phillip Gann was occupied for 40 Days and a Half making of frames for ye Scenes and other work a Bout them at 12:^{d}' per day (II.16). Finally, Fancort and two others spent up to forty-four days on scenery between December 1750 and March 1751, the month in which Gainsborough died. The carpenters also undertook 'non-theatrical' jobs at the Hall: Berrey, as we have seen, worked on the music rooms; Fancort built a bookcase for Mr Skinner's room and repaired the wainscot (II.15[b]), and both Fancort and Gann were employed on a new building, constructing a frame for the roof, working on the interior and making a new pair of gates (II.15[b] and 16).

If carpenters built frames for flats (and also, presumably, any three-dimensional items of scenery required), the frames were covered in cloth by John Newbould, with occasional assistance from his 'man' or 'prentis'. Two bills from Newbould are presented in II.17: the first relates to the period from 6 December 1749 to 21 August 1750 and is headed 'for the plays'; the second covers the shorter period from 8 November 1750 to 29 January 1751 and is marked 'for work for the Plays'. Both bills are addressed to Lord Gainsborough, who died on 21 March 1751, but annotations on the inside and outside indicate that they include all Newbould's demands to Lady Day (25 March). Three of his assistants are named – John Low (29 December 1749), Oliver Clingworth and Thomas Sherman (both 17 December 1750).

The flavour of the entries can be tasted from a number of samples. Newbould covered two frames on 21 August 1750 and '3 frames for the front of ye stage' three months later. On 29 November he covered 'a frame d^o [for the stair case] & 2 frames for windows for the stage', and on 17 December 'a frame & door for the stair case'. He seems to have had difficulty in spelling the word 'scenes'. Side 'sceeings' were fitted by John Low on 29 December 1749, and six side 'sceenngs' were covered by Newbould himself on 8 November 1750. Newbould also fitted 'Chamber sceeings' on 30 December 1749, altered unspecified 'seeings' on 2 January 1750 and made two back 'sceeings' on 19 November. It may be that some of his scenes functioned also as screens and that 'screens' or 'screenings' is occasionally what he meant.

This possibility may be strengthened by references to curtains, for which, also, Newbould was responsible. That there was a stage curtain is clear from an entry for 22 December 1750, a day he spent 'taking the stage Curtain down making it broader & putting it up again'. What is not clear from this entry is whether the curtain was installed at the front of the stage or the back. Other references to curtains are no less difficult to interpret. In December 1749 Newbould made 'a new Curtain' and altered 'the old Curtain'; on 29 November 1750 he charged for 'making Curtains for the hall doors [and] a Curtain for the stair Case', and on 17 December for 'making the hall window Curtains & putting them up'. Meanwhile, he had spent half a day in April 1750 'seaming Cloth to part the barn'. None of these entries mentions a stage, but it appears from their headings that Newbould's bills relate exclusively to work for the plays. The references to the Hall and the barn suggest that these are the places where plays were performed and recall Mrs Smith's statement in 1748 that there were 'Plays acted both in the House, & in the Gardens'.[37] Whatever the venue, some features of the building probably formed part of the set, so it is possible that some of Newbould's curtains acted both as items of scenery and as soft furnishings for the Hall.

Repertory

The bills for the construction of stages and scenery do not mention titles of plays, but the repertory of dramas available at Exton can be inferred from the bills for the purchase and binding of books. These documents identify twenty-four plays – seven by Shakespeare, the remainder by authors active mainly between the Restoration and the accession of George III. Most of the purchases were supplied by Andrew Rogers (II.7), from whom Gainsborough bought copies of five Shakespeare plays (*King Lear*, *Richard III*, *Othello*, *Henry IV Part 2* and *The Merry Wives of Windsor*) and of Nicholas Rowe's *The Fair Penitent* (1702/3), Aaron Hill's *The Walking Statue, or The Devil in the Wine-Cellar* (1709), Joseph Addison's *The Drummer* (1715) and James Thomson's *Edward and Eleonora* (1739). That he bought five copies of *The Cobler* [sic] *of Preston* (1716), by Christopher Bullock or Charles Johnson, and four each of *King Lear*, *Richard III*, *The Drummer* and *Edward and Eleonora* suggests that he intended at least to hold a group reading of these plays, if not to stage them. From John Cooke (II.5) he purchased a copy of George Farquhar's *The Constant Couple, or A Trip to the Jubilee* (1700), two copies of *Double Falsehood* (1728) and one of Tobias Smollett's *The Regicide* (1749). William Shropshire (II.10) supplied two copies of Thomas Southerne's *The Fatal Marriage* (1694) and one of Aaron Hill's *Merope* soon after its publication in 1749.

Gainsborough also paid for many of his purchases to be bound and for approximately half of those to be interleaved – a form of binding in which the pages of a play (or libretto) are separated by blank sheets of paper on which production notes can be written. The binding and interleaving of individual plays were done mostly by Rogers and Benjamin Christian (II.4). Seven plays were bound without interleaving, but only two of them appear from the bills to have been purchased during this period: *Double Falsehood* (bought 2 January 1749; bound 11 December 1750 'for Lady Juliana'; bound and interleaved 5 January 1751) and *The Fatal Marriage* (bought 10 February 1750, bound 1 March). The documents offer no evidence of purchase for *Hamlet*, Thomas Otway's *The Orphan* (1680), Dryden's *The Spanish Fryar, or Double Discovery* (1681) or Nicholas Rowe's *Jane Shore* (1714), all of which Gainsborough had bound.

There is some uncertainty about Aaron Hill's *Athelwold* (1731). Christian made a charge on 13 October 1750 for 'Writing [i.e., copying] the Tragedy of Athelwold' and on 8 November for 'Athelwold bound 2 Vol.^{s} Quarto'; meanwhile, on 26 October Rogers had billed Gainsborough for '½ binding and interleaving *Athelwold*'. It is probable that Christian bound the manuscript copy he had made, while Rogers bound and interleaved a printed edition, but we cannot be sure. In addition to *Athelwold*, twelve other plays were interleaved. Six of them were bought in the period 1748–50: a duodecimo edition of *Othello*, *The Drummer*, *Henry IV Part 2*, *Double Falsehood*, *King Lear* and *The Merry Wives of Windsor*. It is not known how or when the other six were acquired – two more copies of *Othello* (one in octavo), *Henry IV Part 1*, *The Funeral*, *The False Marriage*, *Venice Preserv'd* and *Jane Shore* – but they certainly were available at Exton. That all of them were interleaved means that Gainsborough must at least have considered the possibility of staging them. Perhaps this is the reason why so many were also half- rather than full-bound.

Productions

Notwithstanding the evidence of binding, the strongest indications of dramatic production are found in the bill from Samuel Goodwin, who painted scenes, and in those from John Newbould, who, in addition to supplying scenery, made, altered and repaired costumes and properties. Goodwin claims in his bill (II.2) to have painted the 'Rock Scene' and the 'Garden' in *Athelwold*, the 'Mountain Scene', the 'Wood Scene' and the 'Lodge' in *Double Falsehood*, the 'Inn Yard for Harry ye 4th' and 'The Stone' in *Jane Shore*. Most of these can be identified. For *Athelwold* he must have painted the rocky coast for Act I and either the grove in the palace garden (Acts II and III) or the garden (Act V). The 'mountain scene' in *Double Falsehood* was presumably the 'wide plain, with a prospect of mountains at a distance' (Act IV and V/1), and the 'lodge' 'an apartment in the lodge' (V/2); the 'wood' may have been a substitute for one of the sets in Act I, II or III, which do not appear in Goodwin's list. An 'Inn Yard' at Rochester is the setting for Act II, scene 1, of *Henry IV Part 1*, but 'The Stone' is not prescribed for any scene in *Jane Shore*. Thus, although the bill suggests that these plays were produced, it does not provide proof; furthermore, the fact that Goodwin also painted a new stage, possibly the one built in 1750, is the only clue in his bill as to when these performances might have taken place.

Nothing more is known about the possible production of *Athelwold* or *Jane Shore*, but there is further evidence on *Double Falsehood* and *Henry IV Part 1*. The authorship of *Double Falsehood; or, The Distressed Lovers*, which was first performed at the Drury Lane theatre in 1727, is disputed. The play is related to the lost *Cardenio*, which was derived from an episode in Cervantes' novel *Don Quixote* and has been attributed to Shakespeare and John Fletcher, but in 1728 it was published under the name of Lewis Theobald.[38] In a copy of the second edition, now in the Folger Shakespeare Library, Gainsborough's daughter Juliana Noel wrote her name and the date 10 March 1742.[39] Annotations against the *dramatis personæ* in the same copy show that she and other members of the family participated in a domestic production. Juliana took the role of Violante; Jane, her older sister, that of Leonora. Henriquez was played by their father, Lord Gainsborough; Julio ('in love with Leonora') possibly by their uncle James, and Don Bernard (Leonora's father) by Mr Brown. This last actor may have been the 'John Brown Esq:ᵉ' for whom a coat was shortened by John Newbould in January 1751.[40] Manuscript cuts and alterations to the text and the scene descriptions in Juliana's copy provide evidence of ways in which the play was customised for performance at Exton.[41]

The action revolves around two pairs of lovers and involves disguise and mistaken identity. Apart from love, the principal concerns are truth, honour and the relationship of fathers to children. Leonora cannot resolve whether 'to live without a father's blessing or abandon Julio',[42] and near the end of the play (as printed) the Duke, Henriquez's father, gives voice to the following, strongly held opinion:

> The Voice of Parents is the Voice of Gods:
> For to their Children they are Heav'n's Lieutenants:
> Made Fathers, not for common Uses meerly
> Of Procreation; (Beasts and Birds would be
> As noble then as we are) but to steer
> The wanton Freight of Youth thro' Storms and Dangers,
> Which with full Sails they bear upon: and streighten
> The moral Line of Life, they bend so often.[43]

The first five lines of this speech are reduced to two in Juliana's copy of the play: 'The voice of parents is the voice of Gods: | By Heaven appointed to direct and steer'.[44] If the original text expressed views widely held in the first half of the eighteenth century, the abridged version omits words that presumably were considered unsuitable for the ears of Gainsborough's daughters Jane (aged between 15 and 17, depending on the date of performance) and Juliana (14–16) and of any other young people who might have heard them. The alteration thus casts light on ways in which the potentially delicate topic of relations between parents and children could be addressed at that time.

The text of *Double Falsehood* as printed includes three instructions for music. In Act I, scene 3, Henriquez commands:

> Strike up, my Masters;
> But touch the Strings with a religious Softness;
> Teach Sound to languish thro' the Night's dull Ear,
> 'Till Melancholy start from her lazy Couch,
> And Carelessness grow Convert to Attention.
> [*Musick plays*]

Since there is no indication to the contrary, it may be assumed that the musicians were on stage and that they played quietly while Henriquez continued speaking. Off-stage sounds are called for by the cues '*Flourish within*' and '*Musick within*' in Act III, scene 2, where Leonora urges Julio to 'Hark! again; | These are the Bells knoll for Us'. It would be neat if this tolling were the subject of the bill from Francis Sharp (II.9), but the dates of his bell-ringing seem too widely spaced for the performances of a play.

In Act IV, scene 2, 'Violante *sings within*' and the text of the play gives the words of her song, beginning 'Fond Echo! forego thy light Strain'. The musical setting ('Fond Echo, forbear thy light strain': see Example 2.1) had been composed by 'M.ʳ Gouge' and, under the title *The Forsaken Maid*, had been published three times in 1728–9, with and without a bass line.[45] Since at Exton the role of Violante was taken by Juliana, she presumably sang this song in the production. The nature of the accompaniment is not clear. The play includes the cue '*Lute sounds within*', but an annotation in her copy reveals that the song was 'accompany'd by a Violin con Sordini';[46] perhaps the violin simply doubled the melody.

Juliana's copy of *Double Falsehood* also includes an additional cue for music, from which it emerges that in Act III, scene 2, there was a performance of the 'symphony in Solomon'. This presumably was the movement in Handel's *Solomon* that later became known as 'The Arrival of the Queen of Sheba'. Gainsborough may have attended the first performance of this oratorio, possibly with one or more members of his family.[47] If so, they doubtless enjoyed the symphony, but it is not clear why they should have regarded it as appropriate to this scene in the play. Leonora is due to be married to Henriquez, hopes to be rescued by Julio, and intends – if he does not arrive in time – to stab herself with a dagger that she has hidden in her dress. A

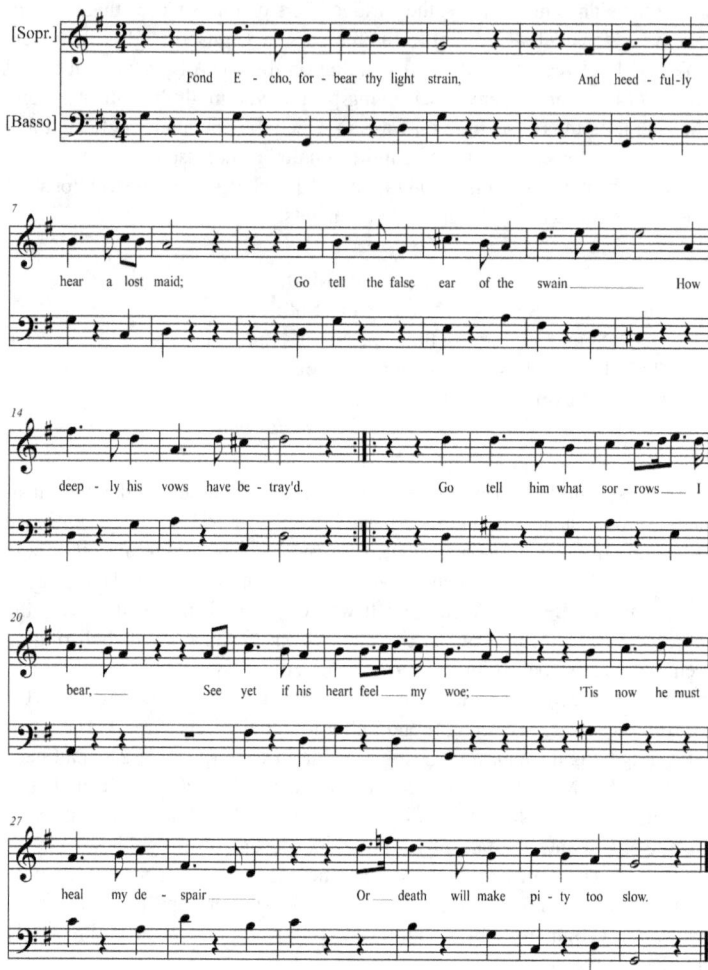

Example 2.1 ['Mr Gouge'], 'Fond Echo, forbear thy light strain', bars 1–32. Transcription from an anonymous song sheet entitled *The Forsaken Maid. A New Song in the Tragedy Call'd* Double Falsehood *by Shakespear* [c. 1728].

scuffle ensues, Leonora swoons and is carried off by servants at the end of the scene. This is all very different from the situation in *Solomon* for which the symphony was composed.

Regardless of the movement's suitability, the cue for this music is important for two further reasons. First, it provides evidence on the date of the production of *Double Falsehood* at Exton. Gainsborough was billed for the purchase of two copies of the play on 2 January 1749 (II.5), but if the production included music from Handel's *Solomon*, it cannot have been staged before the first performance of the oratorio on 17 March. The play is also referred to in bills dated 3 February 1750 for binding and interleaving, 11 December for binding 'for L.^{y} Juliana', and twice on 5 January 1751 – first for interleaving, then for binding (all in II.4). The dates of these entries suggest that *Double Falsehood* was staged in the winter of 1749/50 and/or that of 1750/51; the second of these possibilities is strengthened by the bill for the shortening of the coat for John Brown (II.17[b]).[48] The bill for scene-painting was submitted on 7 June 1751 (II.2), nearly three months after Gainsborough's death and thus well after the play would have been staged. The cue for the symphony is important also because it demonstrates that movements from major works by Handel were used during his lifetime in productions of plays that were mounted by amateurs outside London. At Exton this had already happened on a larger scale in the 1745 and 1748 performances of *Comus*, but this cue in *Double Falsehood* suggests that the practice was far more common than that.

Performances of *Henry IV Part 1* are implied by entries in the bills of John Newbould. These bills, incidentally, are fascinatingly detailed, referring to materials, ribbon, lace and even thread ('thrid'), and specifying amounts and costs of small items. Three of his entries relate to work on the costume and footwear for the character Sir John Falstaff. Falstaff appears in three Shakespeare plays, but only in *Henry IV Part 1* is an inn yard a setting for a scene. On 4 January 1750 Newbould spent 'all day mending sr John Fallstafs dress & getting other dresses ready' (II.17[a]), and on 16 January 1751 he charged for 'altering S:^{r} John Fallstafs boots' and 'altering the breeches'; two days later he mended Falstaff's 'sword scabbard' (II.17[b]). It seems from these entries that *Henry IV Part 1* was performed in January 1750 and 1751.

Newbould also made costumes for characters who cannot be associated with the plays mentioned above – a Corporal (30 December 1749) and a Sailor and a Guard (26 November 1750) – and for Sir Toby Belch in *Twelfth Night*. For this last play the documents provide no evidence of purchase or binding, except in Theobald's edition of Shakespeare's *Works*. On 6 December 1749 Newbould charged for 'making my lord a blue Coate for sr. Toby' and 'making a belley',[49] and three days later for 'making the Clowns dress [costume]'. On 27 March 1750 he took the buttons off Sir Toby's coat and transferred them to 'a scarlet freize waistcoate', and on 29 November he billed Gainsborough for 'new buttoning a Coate for sr: toby' (II.17[b]). The implication of these entries is that there were performances of *Twelfth Night* at Exton in December 1749 and November or December 1750.

*

The bills for stages, sets, scenes, painting, lighting, costumes and properties demonstrate clearly that Gainsborough was willing to spend large sums of money on plays at Exton and suggest that his family valued the productions very highly. Much time and effort went into the preparations for a play, and normal life at the Hall must have been disrupted when these were in progress. Assuming that the bills from Newbould and others have been interpreted correctly, the period around Christmas and New Year appears to have been the time when plays were performed indoors – the counterpart to a summer season of music, some of it outdoors. Gainsborough himself was surely the 'lord' who played Toby Belch in *Twelfth Night* and possibly Falstaff in *Henry IV Part 1*; his young son Lord Campden wore a 'danceing dress' in December 1749, a blue coat in November 1750 and a Page's costume in January 1751, and on 18 January 1751 Newbould made 'lady Juleys [Juliana's] dress'. He also made or altered costumes or coats for eight gentlemen, some of whom, at least, were associated with the family, possibly as members of staff: Mr Blathwait (or Blathwayt: 15 January 1751) had 'known about' music supplied by Smith in 1750 (II.11) and presumably was the 'W Blathwayt' who paid Francis Sharp in 1752 (II.9);[50] Mr [H.] Cumbrey (16 January 1750) was to pay Phillip Gann in 1751 (II.16); he and William Willson (26 November 1750) are named in the poem 'The Bowling-Green' (II.19), and John Brown (7 January 1751) may be the individual referred to there as 'B++n'.[51] The manuscript of poetry (II.18) includes verses referring to characters in *Hamlet, Double Falsehood* and Otway's *The Orphan*, thus suggesting that these plays were produced or read aloud. A final indication that amateur theatricals were a much-loved feature of life at the Hall is provided by the records of binding: Cooke bound '2 vols. of plays, ca[sed and] l[ette]r[e]d' in 1749 (II.5: 17 April), while Christian bound 'A Catalogue of Plays' in 1750 (II.4: 23 February) and 'A Vol. of plays bound in Calf' in 1751 (24 January). That copies of plays were catalogued and bound together suggests that members of the family valued their performances and wanted the evidence of them to be preserved.

Notes

1 For example, Ellen T. Harris, *George Frideric Handel: A Life with Friends* (New York: Norton, 2014), Appendix I: 'Currency, Living Costs, Wages, and Fees'.

2 This information on Shropshire is found in: John Ray, *A Collection of Curious Travels and Voyages [...] Translated from the original High Dutch by Nicholas Staphorst [...]*, 2nd edn (London: Olive Payne [...] and Thomas Woodman [...] and William Shropshire in Old Bond Street, 1738); T[homas] Mozeen, *A Collection of Miscellaneous Essays* (London: for The Author, and sold by Mr. Stuart, Paternoster-Row [...] Mess. Shropshire, in New Bond-street; Mrs. S. Farley, in Castle-Green, Bristol; and Mr. Faulkener, in Dublin, 1762); [Anon.], *An Enquiry into the Rights of the East-India Company of making War and Peace [...]. In a Letter to the Proprietors of East-India Stock. Written in the year 1769. And now first Published* (London: printed for Walter Shropshire in New Bond-street, and Samuel Bladon in Pater-noster Row, 1772).

3   See, for example, Appendix II.5, 1748, entries for 14 May ('Livery Hats'), 11 June ('L.rd Cam.[,] M.r Noel & 2 Serv.ts Hats') and 21 August ('His Lordship 1 Sup.r fine Hat').
4   [Anon.], *Arithmetick made so Easy, that it may be Learned without a Master [...] for the Use of Schools*, trans. Thomas Fletcher (1727), 2nd edn (London: C. Rivington and others, 1740).
5   Gainsborough also paid Arthur Pond 2s. 6d. for 'Anson' and bought a print of him: see above, Chapter 1, note 40.
6   He also translated the librettos of the pasticcio operas *Venceslao* (1731) and *Catone* (1732): see Colin Timms, 'Handel Translators: Humphreys, Oldmixon and Anonymous', *Händel-Jahrbuch*, 70 (2024).
7   Presumably Homer's *Odyssey* was in the translation by Pope and included all five volumes. Gainsborough also subscribed to one of the volumes (see below, Appendix I, 1726).
8   These purchases are presumably additional to acquisitions by subscription – those of Gainsborough's wife to James Thomson's *The Seasons* (1730) and of his sisters, Susanna, Countess of Shaftesbury, and Lady Catherine Noel to John Hughes's *Poems on Several Occasions, with some Select Essays in Prose*, 2 vols. (1735) – a volume to which a Mrs Susan Noel also subscribed.
9   See Richard Leppert, *Music and Image: Domesticity, Ideology and Socio-Cultural Formation in Eighteenth-Century England*, paperback edn (Cambridge: Cambridge University Press, 1993), 51–2.
10 On the subject of education in the eighteenth century see Anthony Fletcher, *Growing Up in England: The Experience of Childhood 1600–1914* (New Haven: Yale University Press, 2008), and *Educating the Child in Enlightenment Britain: Beliefs, Cultures, Practices*, ed. Mary Hilton and Jill Shefrin (Farnham: Ashgate, 2009). See also Amanda Vickery, *The Gentleman's Daughter: Women's Lives in Georgian England* (New Haven: Yale University Press, 1998).
11 See Chapter 1, note 15.
12 Mark Girouard, *Life in the English Country House* (New Haven: Yale University Press, 1978), 179–80.
13 John Brewer, *The Pleasures of the Imagination: English Culture in the Eighteenth Century* (Abingdon: Routledge, 2013), 391.
14 See Ruth Smith, *Charles Jennens: The Man behind Handel's* Messiah (London: Handel House Trust and Gerald Coke Handel Foundation, 2012), and Brenda Sumner, 'Charles Jennens' Piano and Music Room', *Handel Institute Newsletter*, 22/2 (2011), [1–3].
15 As suggested by the occupations specified in Thomas Mortimer, *The Universal Director; or, The Nobleman and Gentleman's True Guide to the Masters and Professors of the Liberal and Polite Arts and Sciences and of the Mechanic Arts, Manufactures, and Trades* [...], 2 vols. (London: J. Coote, 1763).
16 *The New Grove Dictionary of Music and Musicians*, 2nd edn, ed. Stanley Sadie and John Tyrrell, 29 vols. (London: Macmillan, 2001), *s.v.* Wamsley [Walmsley, Warmsley], Peter.
17 'The Orchestra was full': Martyn to the 4th Earl of Shaftesbury, 1 August 1748, in Betty Matthews, 'Unpublished Letters concerning Handel', *Music & Letters*, 40 (1959), 266; *George Frideric Handel: Collected Documents*, ed. Donald Burrows, Helen Coffey, John Greenacombe and Anthony Hicks, 6 vols. (Cambridge: Cambridge University Press, 2013–), iv, 589, and Colin Timms, 'Handel and *Comus* at Exton', in *New Perspectives on Handel's Music: Essays in Honour of Donald Burrows*, ed. David Vickers (Woodbridge: Boydell, 2022), 261.
18 See Cheryll Duncan, *Felice Giardini and Professional Music Culture in Mid-Eighteenth-Century London* (Royal Musical Association Monographs 35)

(Abingdon: Routledge, 2020), especially Chapter 5 ('Giardini's Account at Cox's Music Shop') and Appendix 1.

19 Michael Talbot, 'From Giovanni Stefano Carbonelli to John Stephen Carbonell: A Violinist turned Vintner in Handel's London', *Göttinger Händel-Beiträge*, 14 (2012), 265–99. Charles Burney, in *A General History of Music from the Earliest Ages to the Present Period*, ed. Frank Mercer, 2 vols. (London: G. T. Foulis, 1935), ii, 729, described Rutland as 'a nobleman who, by study and application, had rendered himself a most intelligent judge both of the theory and practice of the art of Music'.

20 Talbot, 'From Giovanni Stefano Carbonelli to John Stephen Carbonell', 274.

21 For the reasoning see Appendix II, especially the Commentaries to II.5, 7 and 11.

22 The complete title page is quoted in Frank Kidson, 'James Oswald, Dr. Burney, and "The Temple of Apollo"', *The Musical Antiquary*, 2 (1910–11), 35.

23 See Roger Fiske, *English Theatre Music in the Eighteenth Century*, 2nd edn (Oxford: Oxford University Press, 1986), 229–33.

24 See John Purser, *Scotland's Music: A History of the Traditional and Classical Music of Scotland from the Earliest Times to the Present Day* (Edinburgh: Mainstream, 1992), 173–88, and *The New Grove Dictionary*, s.v. Oswald, James.

25 See Thomas L. Hankins and Robert J. Silverman, *Instruments and Imagination* (Princeton: Princeton University Press, 1995), 91–2.

26 In addition to the publications mentioned above in notes 22 and 24 see Percy A. Scholes, *The Great Dr. Burney: His Life – His Travels – His Works – His Family and His Friends*, 2 vols. (London: Oxford University Press, 1948), i, 54–7; Fiske, *English Theatre Music*, 222–3, and Hankins and Silverman, *Instruments and Imagination*, 92–3. For Greene's academy see Matthew Gardner, Gardner, *Handel and Maurice Greene's Circle at the Apollo Academy* (Göttingen: V&R unipress, 2008).

27 *Memoirs of Doctor Burney, arranged from his Own Manuscripts, from Family Papers, and from Personal Recollections*, ed. Madame d'Arblay [Fanny Burney], 3 vols. (London: Edward Moxon, 1832), i, 20.

28 Though usually referred to as John Christopher Smith senior, he seems never to have used the name 'John': see Donald Burrows, 'Do we need "John"?', *Handel Institute Newsletter*, 30/1 (2019), [3].

29 *Handel: Collected Documents* (see note 17), iv, 743–4.

30 For details of the Sharp family and their activities see Brian Crosby, 'Private Concerts on Land and Water: The Musical Activities of the Sharp Family, c. 1750–c. 1790', *Royal Musical Association Research Chronicle*, 34 (2001), 1–118, and Hester Grant, *The Good Sharps: The Eighteenth-Century Family that Changed Britain* (London: Vintage, 2021). For information on Zoffany see: *Johan Zoffany RA: Society Observed*, ed. Martin Postle (New Haven: Yale University Press, 2011); Mary Webster, *Johan Zoffany, 1733–1810* (New Haven: Yale University Press, 2011); Penelope Treadwell, *Johan Zoffany: Artist and Adventurer* (London: Paul Holberton, 2009) and *Handel: A Celebration of his Life and Times*, ed. Jacob Simon, 246–7 and painting opposite page 153.

31 Gerard Noel, *Sir Gerard Noel MP and the Noels of Chipping Campden and Exton* (Chipping Campden: Campden and District Historical and Archaeological Society, 2004), 46.

32 See David Coke and Alan Borg, *Vauxhall Gardens: A History* (New Haven: Yale University Press, 2011), especially 56–7 and 141–2.

33 See Handel and Arne, *Comus*, ed. Colin Timms (London: Novello, 2016), p. v, and Timms, 'Handel and *Comus* at Exton', 254–60.

34 See Matthews, 'Unpublished Letters', 264–5; *Handel: Collected Documents*, iv, 322–4, and Timms, 'Handel and *Comus* at Exton', 248–51.

35 See Matthews, 'Unpublished Letters', 266–7; *Handel: Collected Documents*, iv, 588–90, and Timms, 'Handel and *Comus* at Exton', 261–63. 'Mrs Noel' may have been the Susan Noel who had subscribed to Hughes' *Poems on several Occasions* (see above, note 8).
36 According to Harris, *George Frideric Handel* (see note 1), 376, this was the 'daily wage *without drink* for a carpenter, wheelwright, or mason' in 1732. This would have bought one copy of the wordbook for a Handel oratorio.
37 See above, Introduction, p. 2.
38 The question of authorship is discussed in Lewis Theobald, *Double Falsehood*, ed. Brean Hammond (London: Arden Shakespeare, 2010), 76–105, by Robert D. Hume and Jean I. Marsden in Chapters 2 and 4, respectively, of *Revisiting Shakespeare's Lost Play: 'Cardenio/Double Falsehood' in the Eighteenth Century*, ed. Deborah C. Payne (Cham, Switzerland: Palgrave Macmillan, [2016]), and by Naseem Alotaibi, 'Lewis Theobald's *Double Falsehood*: The Authorship Question Reconsidered', PhD dissertation (University of Liverpool, 2016).
39 Lewis Theobald, *Double Falshood; or, The Distrest Lovers*, 2nd edn (London: John Watts, 1728): Washington DC, Folger Shakespeare Library, Prompt D36, endpaper.
40 See Appendix II.17[b].
41 Annotations in Juliana's copy, and their implications, are discussed in Theobald, *Double Falsehood*, ed. Hammond, 117–18.
42 Theobald, *Double Falshood* (1728), Act II, scene 3 (p. 20).
43 Ibid., Act V, scene 2 (pp. 56–7).
44 Theobald, *Double Falsehood*, ed. Hammond, 118.
45 Gouge's first name (or initial) is unknown. 'Fond Echo' was attributed to him in *The Merry Musician*, ii (1728) and *The Musical Miscellany*, ii (1729); see Theobald, *Double Falsehood*, ed. Hammond, 14 (reproduction of *The Musical Miscellany*) and 334–5 (discussion). At least seven other songs by Gouge were published separately or in *Mercurius musicus* (London, 1699–1709) or George Bickham's *Musical Entertainer* (London, 1737–40): see Edith B. Schnapper, *The British Union-Catalogue of Early Music Printed before the Year 1801*, 2 vols. (London: Butterworths Scientific Publications, 1957), i, 107 and 391; ii, 772–3, and the online Répertoire International des Sources Musicales (RISM).
46 Theobald, *Double Falsehood*, ed. Hammond, 118.
47 See above, p. 18.
48 See above, p. 46.
49 Either literally a belly, so as to render Sir Toby corpulent, or some kind of bag or purse.
50 He is probably not to be identified with the William Blathwayt (1719–87) of Dyrham Park, Gloucestershire, whose uncle John (1690–1752) was an outstanding young harpsichordist before joining the army and becoming a colonel: see H. Diack Johnstone, 'John Blathwayt: A Musical British Teenager on the Grand Tour', *The Musical Times*, 162 (summer 2021), 27–47.
51 Mr Proby (2 January 1750), Mr Hurst and Mr Snow (both 3 January), Robert Pragnell (26 November 1750) and William Moulten (29 November) have not been identified.

# 3   Gainsborough's Legacy

Henry IV Part 1 is the last theatrical or musical work for which there is evidence of performance at Exton (in January 1751) during the lifetime of the 4th Earl of Gainsborough. It may also have been the last such performance at the Hall for some time. Baptist Noel was succeeded in March 1751 by his son Baptist, Viscount Campden, who was ten years old at the time and died eight years later. Although the 5th Earl had appeared on stage in *Comus* (possibly in 1745, certainly in 1748) and seems to have sung in *Samson* (in 1750), the brevity of his tenure of the title, not to mention his youth, gave him little opportunity – even if he had the ambition – to build on his boyhood experiences of music and theatre or to continue the series of artistic projects that had been initiated by his father. Any incentive to follow in the footsteps of the 4th Earl may also have evaporated in November 1756, when his widowed mother married his father's cousin, Thomas Noel MP, of Walcot, Northamptonshire. The young Baptist was succeeded in 1759 by his sixteen-year-old brother Henry, who held the title of 6th Earl of Gainsborough for nearly forty years.

Henry had a special interest in the natural world and above all in plants.[1] His improvements to the estate are documented by his botanical notebooks and by numerous bills for the purchase of pots, seeds and plants of all kinds, including shrubs and trees. At Exton he built a hothouse, established a herbarium and created a botanical garden. He was made an Honorary Fellow of the Linnean Society in 1788, the year of its foundation, and in the same year he engaged William Legg of Stamford to design and construct a folly beside the lake on the estate; known as Fort Henry, this building still stands. After the death of Thomas Noel, also in 1788, Henry commissioned Joseph Nollekens to create the large monument to his father (the 4th Earl), his mother (Elizabeth, *née* Chapman, who had died in 1771) and her second husband (Thomas Noel) that is still to be seen in Exton parish church.[2] Having never married, however, the 6th Earl left no heir, and the title died with him in 1798.[3]

Henry was dearly loved by his sisters.[4] Like him, Elizabeth, Anne and Mary Noel remained unmarried and continued to live in or near Exton beyond the turn of the century; Sophia, their youngest sister, married in 1773 and died seven years later. Elizabeth was 'a botanist of some distinction' and also a botanical artist who contributed to the *English Botany* of J. E. Smith, founder of the Linnean Society.⁵ The siblings were not uninterested in other arts. Henry subscribed to John Parry's *Collection of Welsh, English and Scottish Airs* (1761), Catherine Jemmat's *Miscellanies, in Prose and Verse* (1766) and Samuel Long's *Four Lessons and Two Voluntarys for the Harpsichord or Organ* (1770) – an intriguing assortment.⁶ The publication of Long's *Four Lessons* was also supported by Henry's sisters. Elizabeth, who as a teenager had taken part in *Comus*, had already bought into Joseph Eyre's *Eight Sonatas in Three Parts, Six for Two Violins, and Two for Two German Flutes, and a Bass* in *c*. 1765, the year in which a 'Miss Noel' had stumped up for the publication of Samuel Wise's *Six Lessons for the Harpsichord*. Elizabeth also subscribed to John Pixell's *Odes, Cantatas, Songs, &c., Divine, Moral, Entertaining* [...], op. 2 (1775) and to James Brooks's *Second Sett of Twelve Glees for Three and Four Voices* (*c*. 1798), while her sister Mary helped finance the publication of Jane Mary Guest's *Six Sonatas for the Harpsichord or Piano Forte* [...], op. 1 (*c*. 1783).

Any study of music and theatre in eighteenth-century Exton must take account of three factors that date from the early nineteenth century. The first is 'the extensive fire that virtually destroyed' Exton Hall in 1810.⁷ It was thought for a long time that the library and the Noel family archives had been consumed by these flames, but in 1987 a substantial collection of records was found to have survived in rusty deed boxes in the stables and the muniment room. This is the collection that was deposited in ROLLR and later supplemented with additions. Although it is the 'largest single family collection' that this record office has ever received⁸ (it now occupies nearly 700 boxes), it does not include every document about the Noels at Exton that has ever existed: there is 'virtually no family correspondence', for example, dating from before the late eighteenth century.⁹

The other two factors are known from publications. Ten years after the fire, the following paragraph was published in a letter to the *Gentleman's Magazine*:¹⁰

> *En passant*, Mr. Urban, I wish to inquire whether any documents can be supplied or referred to, respecting those noble fetes or galas that were formerly given, about 60 or 70 years ago, at Exton in Rutland, by the then Earl of Gainsborough, who might be entitled the Mæcenas of his age? One or two ladies of that noble family are said still to survive in that neighbourhood; and if, by their means, or any other, any materials on so entertaining a subject could be pointed out, they might be somewhat augmented by the present inquirer.
>
> Yours, &c. EREUNETES.

If 'Ereunetes' had written '70 to 75' years ago, rather than '60 or 70', his estimate of the date would have been completely accurate. Nevertheless, he must have been referring to the 4th Earl – the only eighteenth-century Earl of Gainsborough who could be described as a Mæcenas – and to the lavish entertainments that he organised at Exton in the 1740s and 1750. The 'ladies' of his family still living in the neighbourhood must have been his daughters Anne (born 1737), who died at North Luffenham in 1825, and Mary (born 1744), who was living in the same village in 1803 and died in 1820. If the correspondent possessed some materials relating to these entertainments, as his final clause suggests, it would be interesting to know what they were. The main point, however, is that by harking back to the 4th Earl's 'noble fetes or galas' he inadvertently confirmed that no entertainment promoted by the 5th or 6th Earl had made such an impact or remained so long in the memory.

The paragraph quoted above was mentioned by John Crosse in 1825, in his *Sketch of the Rise and Progress of Musical Festivals in Great Britain*:[11]

> The latter nobleman [the Earl of Abingdon] expended £1600. in support of Bach and Abel's concerts, and the Earl of Gainsborough enlisted many of the neighbouring families as members of an *Academy of Music*, at Exton in Rutlandshire, respecting the proceedings of which an inquiry was made in the *Gentleman's Magazine* for August, 1820, and the papers relating to which, with the signatures of the principal parties, fell into our possession at the dispersion of the fine collection of music that belonged to the Society, a few years ago.

This is intriguing. Crosse declares that an Earl of Gainsborough had an 'Academy of Music' at Exton that included members of neighbouring families, and that this ensemble possessed a 'fine collection of music'. Given his reference to the concerts of Johann Christian Bach and Carl Friedrich Abel, the Earl of Gainsborough in question must have been the 6th, in which case Crosse would have erred in connecting his Academy of Music with the enquiry in the *Gentleman's Magazine*. One explanation that would link this academy to the 'noble fetes and galas' promoted by the 4th Earl – and vindicate Crosse – is the possibility that the 6th Earl's academy was a continuation or reincarnation of an ensemble that had been founded by his father and had performed in his entertainments until at least the summer of 1750. That this is not inconceivable is suggested by Jenny Clark's statement that 'the intimate connection between Hall and village is well-documented'.[12]

Moreover, similar developments were taking place elsewhere.[13] At Spalding, about twenty-five miles north-east of Exton, concerts involving professional and amateur musicians formed part of the proceedings of the Gentlemen's Society, of which the membership included William Noel, MP for Stamford (1722–47), Charles Jennens and the composer Musgrave Heighington.[14] The society's Anniversary Ode in 1739, which was written by Heighington, began with an overture but essentially comprised 'a three-part chorus, repeated at the end, in between which each member of the Heighington family sung a verse, firstly Heighington himself, followed by his wife and son'.[15] The overall structure of this composition seems very similar to that of Handel's finale to *Comus*, which was sung by Gainsborough and two of his daughters: maybe Gainsborough was aware of Heighington's work – he subscribed to his *Six Select Odes* [1745] – and suggested that a similar design should be adopted for the conclusion of the masque. In the second half of the century, at Wombourne (south-west of Wolverhampton), music-making was the driving passion of the local squire Samuel Hellier (1736–84), an amateur violinist who started collecting music at Oxford in the 1750s and eventually amassed a substantial amount, mostly of printed editions. In addition to music, he also acquired a considerable number of musical instruments which he encouraged his estate workers to play, thus exhibiting a laudable concern 'to further the capacity of [his] employees for cultural advancement'.[16]

The end of Crosse's statement raises another intriguing question. If the academy's music collection was dispersed 'a few years ago', presumably in or just after 1820, and its 'papers' fell into Crosse's possession at the same time, one wonders whether this music and these papers constituted the materials to which 'Ereunetes' had access and whether 'Ereunetes' was actually Crosse himself. Furthermore, if the music and papers were in his possession when his *Sketch* [...] *of Musical Festivals* was published (1825), where were they kept before their 'dispersion'? The obvious answer to this question – if the 6th Earl was involved with the academy and if the papers really did bear 'the signatures of the principal parties' – is Exton Hall, in which case the music and papers (or a sizable proportion of them) would have escaped the fire at the house in 1810 and their loss or destruction (assuming they no longer exist) would have occurred after 1820.

*

Since the documents in Appendix II relate mainly to the late 1740s and early 1750s, they do not furnish evidence of cultural activity at Exton during the earlier decades of the 4th Earl of Gainsborough and may therefore give a somewhat misleading impression of life at the Hall during the period of his tenure as a whole. Nevertheless, they do provide a reliable basis for a number of conclusions. As we have seen, plays were produced in the summers of 1741 and 1742, and probably earlier;[17] the Noels cultivated music long before the earliest of the bills, and Baptist Noel's interest in the art is documented from the mid-1720s.[18] In the late 1730s and early 1740s several factors appear to have come together, culminating in Handel's visit to Exton in 1745 and the performances of *Comus*. These factors include: the desire nurtured by Gainsborough's brother James Noel, by his brother-in-law the 4th Earl of Shaftesbury, by Shaftesbury's cousin James Harris and possibly by others, that Handel should compose more settings of texts by John Milton; the success in London of Arne's setting of Dalton's *Comus*, adapted from Milton; the fact that this masque was the only major poem by Milton that had been written with music in mind but not yet set by Handel, and the fact that the oldest of Gainsborough's daughters had reached an age when they could participate with understanding in a production of a work that extols resistance to pleasures of the flesh. If the staging of *Comus* in 1745 demonstrates Gainsborough's interest in Milton and contemporary musical theatre, the presence of Handel seems to symbolise the earl's wish that the composer be involved in the music for the entertainment. Be that as it may, Handel's visit to Exton must have boosted Gainsborough's admiration for the composer and reinforced his own artistic ambitions, and it may also have provided the impetus for him in about 1747 to buy the bust of Handel that is mentioned in a letter and bill from Roubiliac.[19] When *Comus* was revived in 1748, the staging may have been more elaborate than in 1745, and the first of the performances was followed by a rendition of *Deborah*.

Comus appears to be the only piece of musical theatre of which Gainsborough staged a production. Although incidental music was included in some of the dramas produced at Exton, it seems that, after 1748, music and plays were performed separately: broadly speaking, summer was the season for music, Christmas and New Year the period for plays. In December 1749 and January 1750 there appear to have been productions of *Twelfth Night* and *Henry IV Part 1*, a coupling apparently repeated roughly twelve months later; in the winter of 1749/50 and/or 1750/51 there seems also to have been a production of Theobald's *Double Falsehood*. In the meantime, in August–September 1750, there was a music festival in which there were performances of Handel's *Alexander's Feast*, *Samson* and the funeral anthem *The Ways of Zion do mourn*. It is clear that Gainsborough had an interest in the composer and possessed a fair amount of his music, both printed and manuscript, but it is equally clear from his subscriptions to publications that his musical interests also extended to others, not least to native British composers. From the available documents it appears that Gainsborough, unlike Shaftesbury and Jennens, had no ambition to amass a comprehensive collection of Handel's works. By contrast, he seems to have been interested above all in encouraging the performance of music and drama for entertainment and instruction and in enriching by this means the education and experience of his family and guests.

If Gainsborough had lived longer, the pattern of performance might have become firmer and the music festival have grown larger. Even so, he would probably have tried to avoid engaging professional musicians and continued to cultivate the amateur performance of music and plays, in line with a belief in the educational and social – not to mention medical – value of the arts. Married in 1728, he appears to have started encouraging performance in the 1740s, when his children would have been starting to acquire some proficiency in music. The proof of his commitment, provided by documents in ROLLR, admittedly dates from a brief period, yet it is abundantly clear that the period 1745–50 was the high point for music and theatre in eighteenth-century Exton and that Gainsborough was the driving force behind it. Perhaps these are the reasons why he was referred to as the 'Great Earl' in the poem

'The Bowling-Green' (II.19). They certainly explain why the entertainments promoted by the 4th Earl of Gainsborough were still being remembered in the early nineteenth century and should not be forgotten today.

Notes

1. Gerard Noel, *Sir Gerard Noel MP and the Noels of Chipping Campden and Exton* (Chipping Campden: Campden and District Historical and Archaeological Society, 2004), 207–8.
2. 'There are no churches in Rutland and few in England in which English sculpture from the C16 to the C18 can be studied so profitably and enjoyed so much as at Exton': Nikolaus Pevsner, *Leicestershire and Rutland*, revised Elizabeth Williamson with Geoffrey K. Brandwood, 2nd edn (Harmondsworth: Penguin, 1984), 468–9.
3. The title was recreated in 1841.
4. Emilia F. Noel, *Some Letters and Records of the Noel Family* (London: St Catherine Press, 1910), 24.
5. Noel, *Sir Gerard Noel MP*, 207. See James Edward Smith, *English Botany*, 36 vols. (London: The Author, 1790–1814). Smith's name does not appear in volumes 1–3, which were published under that of the naturalist James Sowerby.
6. These and the following subscriptions appear in the online Dataset of Subscribers to Eighteenth-Century Music Publications in Britain and Ireland, by Simon D. I. Fleming and Martin Perkins (2022; accessed 11 July 2023).
7. Noel, *Sir Gerard Noel MP*, 168.
8. Jenny Clark, 'Family Annals: The Exton Manuscripts', *Rutland Record*, 13 (1993), 118.
9. Clark, 'Family Annals', 123.
10. *The Gentleman's Magazine*, 90/2 (August, 1820), 102. Sylvanus Urban was the pseudonym of Edward Cave.
11. John Crosse, *An Account of the Grand Musical Festival, held in September, 1823, in the Cathedral Church of York [...] to which is prefixed, A Sketch of the Rise and Progress of Musical Festivals in Great Britain; with Biographical and Historical Notes* (York: John Wolstenholme, 1825), 230–31, note.
12. Clark, 'Family Annals', 121–2.
13. See, for example, *The Eighteenth Century* (The Blackwell History of Music in Britain, 4), ed. H. Diack Johnstone and Roger Fiske (Oxford: Blackwell, 1990), and *Music in the British Provinces 1690–1914*, ed. Rachel Cowgill and Peter Holman (Aldershot: Ashgate, 2007).
14. Simon D. I. Fleming, 'The Musical Activities of the Spalding Gentlemen's Society', *Royal Musical Association Research Chronicle*, 48 (2017), 67 and 89. William Noel may have been the 'Hon. Mr. Noel' who, like the 4th Earl of Gainsborough, subscribed to the publication of Heighington's *Six Select Odes of Anacreon in Greek and Six of Horace in Latin* [1745]. The York musician John Hebden, to whose *Six Concertos in Seven Parts*, op. 2 [1745], Gainsborough also subscribed, was in Stamford in 1739 and 1745: see Fleming, 'The Musical Activities', 76.
15. Fleming, 'The Musical Activities', 73 and 85.
16. Percy Young, 'The Shaw-Hellier Collection', in *Handel Collections and Their History*, ed. Terence Best (Oxford: Clarendon Press, 1993), 158–70, at 161. For the music see Ian Ledsham, *A Catalogue of the Shaw-Hellier Collection in the Music Library, Barber Institute of Fine Arts, the University of Birmingham* (Aldershot: Ashgate, 1999). The instruments are in the Musical Instruments Museums at the University of Edinburgh; for details see Catherine Frew and Arnold Myers, 'Sir

Samuel Hellier's "Musicall Instruments"', *Galpin Society Journal*, 56 (2003), 6–26 and 186–9. For an account of Hellier's music-making see Martin Perkins, 'Music in Country Houses of the English Midlands, 1750–1810', 2 vols., PhD dissertation (Birmingham City University, 2020/21), i, 265–93.

17 See Introduction, p. 2.
18 See Chapter 1, p. 13.
19 For the document and for secondary literature see Appendix II.14.

Appendix I
Subscriptions and Dedications

This Appendix lists printed books and music to which the 4th Earl of Gainsborough, his wife (the countess) and his mother (the dowager countess) subscribed. It also lists one book that was dedicated to him and two that were dedicated to his wife; these are identified below by the word 'dedication'. His mother's subscriptions are included because they occurred at a time when her son would have been old enough to be aware of them. The section devoted to Gainsborough is divided into two subsections – Books and Music; the other two sections are not. In every section and subsection the works are presented in chronological order of publication. While every attempt has been made to ensure that the lists are complete, it is possible that some items have nevertheless been missed.

Baptist Noel, 4th Earl of Gainsborough

Books

[1725]   Giovanni Boccaccio, *Il Decameron* [...] *Del MDXXVII* ([Londra:] Tommaso Edlin).
1725   [Mary] Davys, *The Works of Mrs. Davys: consisting of Plays, Novels, Poems and Familiar Letters*, 2 vols. (London: The Author).
1726   Homer, *The Odyssey of Homer. Translated from the Greek* [by Alexander Pope], vol. 5 (London: Bernard Lintot).
1726   *Miscellaneous Poems and Translations. By several Hands*, ed. Richard Savage (London: Samuel Chapman). Gainsborough's wife also subscribed to this anthology (see below).
1727   Baldassar Castiglione, *Il cortegiano, or The Courtier* [...] *and A New Version of the Same into English. Together with several of his Celebrated Pieces, as well Latin as Italian, both in Prose and Verse. To which is prefix'd the Life of the Author by A. P. Castiglione, of the same Family* (London: The Editor).
1729   Richard Browne, *Medicina Musica: or, A Mechanical Essay on the Effects of Singing, Musick, and Dancing, on Human Bodies. Revis'd and corrected. To which is annex'd A New Essay on the Nature and Cure of the Spleen and Vapours* (Uppingham: John Cooke). Dedication.
1729   John Cheny, *An Historical List of all Horse-Matches Run* [...] *in 1729* (London: s. n.). Gainsborough also subscribed to the editions of 1731, 1738, 1739 and 1744.
1732   Duncan Campbel, *Secret Memoirs of the late Mr Duncan Campbel, the famous Deaf and Dumb Gentleman* (London: J. Millan and J. Chrichley).

62 *Appendix I*

1732–5 Frances Peck, *Desiderata curiosa: or, A Collection of Divers Scarce and Curious Pieces (Relating Chiefly to Matters of English History) in Six Books* (London: s. n.).
1733 *The Practical Husbandman and Planter; or, Observations on the Ancient and Modern Husbandry, Planting, Gardening, &c.* [...] *by a Society of Husbandmen and Planters*, vol. 1 (Cambridge and London: S. Switzer).
1734 Gilbert Burnet, *Bishop Burnet's History of his Own Time*, vol. 2: *From the Revolution to the Conclusion of the Treaty of Peace of Utrecht* (London: The Editor).
1738 Thomas Oughton, *Ordo judiciorum; sive, Methodus procedendi in negotiis et litibus in foro ecclesiastico-civili Britannico et Hibernico*, [vol. 1] (London: J. Hooke).
1738 Oughton, *Ordo judiciorum; seu, Formularium in negotiis et litibus in foro ecclesiastico-civili Britannico et Hibernico*, vol. 2 (London: The Author).
1742 Castiglione, *Il cortegiano*, 2nd edn [see above, 1727].
1743 Thomas Birch, *The Heads of Illustrious Persons of Great Britain, Engraven by Mr. Houbraken, and Mr. Vertue, with their Lives and Characters* (London: John and Paul Knapton).
1746–8 [Plautus, Titus Maccius], *Mr. Cooke's Edition and Translation of the Comedys of Plautus*, vol. 1 (London: J. Purser).[1]
1747 John Roque, *A New and Accurate Plan of the Cities of London and Westminster, and Borough of Southwark, with contiguous Buildings, Engraved by John Pine*.[2]
1748 [Mary] Leapor, *Poems upon Several Occasions. By Mrs. Leapor of Brackley in Northamptonshire* (London: J. Roberts).
1748 Thomas Rutherforth, *A System of Natural Philosophy, Being a Course of Lectures in Mechanics, Optics, Hydrostatics, and Astronomy which are read in St Johns College Cambridge*, 2 vols. (Cambridge: W. Thurlbourn).
1749 Anne Thérèse de Marguenat de Courcelles, Marchioness de Lambert, *Letters to her Son and Daughter on True Education &c. &c. &c. Translated by Mr. Rowell* (London: M. Cooper).[3]
1749 John Milton, *Paradise Lost. A Poem, in Twelve Books.* [...] *A New Edition, with Notes of Various Authors, by Thomas Newton, D. D.*, 2 vols. (London: J. and R. Tonson and S. Draper).
1750 Archibald Bower, *The History of the Popes from the Foundation of the See of Rome to the Present Time*, 7 vols. (London: the Author, 1748–66). Gainsborough subscribed to vol. 2.

Music

1724 Attilio Ariosti, *Alla Maestà di Giorgio Rè della Gran Britagna, &c: &c:* [Six Cantatas and Six Lessons for the Viola d'Amore] (London: s. n.).
1725 *A Pocket Companion for Gentlemen and Ladies. Being a Collection of Favourite Songs out of the Most Celebrated Opera's compos'd by Mr. Handel, Bononcini, Attilio* [Ariosti], *&c. to which is added several Choice Songs of Mr. Handel's, never before printed*, vol. 2 (London: J. Cluer and B. Creake). Gainsborough's mother also subscribed to this edition (see below).
1731 Michael Christian Festing, *Twelve Sonata's in Three Parts*, op. 2 (London: Printed by William Smith [...] and Sold only by the Author).[4] Gainsborough's wife also subscribed to this edition (see below).

1737	George Bickham, *The Musical Entertainer*, vol. 1 (London: George Bickham). Issue 21: dedication.
1737	Charles Maclean, *Twelve Solo's or Sonatas for a Violin and Violoncello, with a Thorough Bass for Harpsichord*, op. 1 (Edinburgh: The Author).[5]
[1745]	Musgrave Heighington, *Six Select Odes of Anacreon in Greek and Six of Horace in Latin* (London: John Simpson).[6]
[1745]	John Hebden, *Six Concertos in Seven Parts for Four Violins, a Tenor Violin, a Violoncello with a Thorough Bass for the Harpsicord [...] Opera II^a* (London: The Author).
1747	William Boyce, *Twelve Sonatas for Two Violins, with a Bass for the Violoncello or Harpsicord* (London: I. Walsh, for the Author).[7]
[1747]	Festing, *Six Solos for a Violin and Thorough-Bass* [...] op. 7 (London: William Smith).

Dorothy Noel (*née* Manners), Dowager Countess of Gainsborough

1720	Henry Cornwall, *Observations upon Several Voyages to India out and Home* (London: The Author). Subscribed to by 'The Lady Gainsborough'.
1725	*A Pocket Companion for Gentlemen and Ladies. Being a Collection of Favourite Songs out of the Most Celebrated Opera's compos'd by Mr. Handel, Bononcini, Attilio* [Ariosti], *&c. to which is added several Choice Songs of Mr. Handel's, never before printed*, vol. 2 (London: J. Cluer and B. Creake). The 4th Earl also subscribed to this edition (see above).
1727	David Scott, *The History of Scotland [...] from the Year of the World 3619 to the Year of Christ 1726* (London: J. Cluer and A. Campbell).

Elizabeth Noel (*née* Chapman), Countess of Gainsborough

1726	*Miscellaneous Poems and Translations. By several Hands*, ed. Richard Savage (London: Samuel Chapman). Elizabeth's husband also subscribed to this edition (see above).
1729	Anne Thérèse de Marguenat de Courcelles, *Advice from a Mother to her Son and Daughter. Written originally in French by the Marchioness de Lambert [...] Done into English by a Gentleman* [William Hatchett] (London: Thomas Worrall). Dedication. The countess subscribed to a later edition: *A New-Year's-Gift, being Advice from a Mother [...]* (Dublin: George Risk and others, 1740).
1730	James Thomson, *The Seasons* (London: s. n.).
1730	Michael Christian Festing, *Twelve Solo's for a Violin and Thorough Bass*, op. 1 (London: William Smith).
1731	Festing, *Twelve Sonata's in Three Parts*, op. 2 (London: Printed by William Smith [...] and Sold only by the Author). Elizabeth's husband also subscribed to this edition (see above).
1734	Mary Barber, *Poems on Several Occasions* (London: C. Rivington). The countess also subscribed also to editions of 1735 and 1736.
[1738]	George Frideric Handel, *Alexander's Feast, or The Power of Music* (London: John Walsh). The same list of subscribers appeared in the reprint of the work (1739).

1746   William Weston, *The Moral Impossibility of Conquering England. And the Absurdity of the Dispensing Power of the Pope. Three Sermons preached during the Progress of the Rebellion*, 2nd edn (Cambridge: W. Thurlbourn; London: J. and P. Knapton and others). Dedication.

1746–8   [Plautus, Titus Maccius], *Mr. Cooke's Edition and Translation of the Comedys of Plautus*, vol. 1 (London: J. Purser).

Notes

1. Gainsborough subscribed to a Royal Paper edition. His wife, the countess, also subscribed. Cf. *George Frideric Handel: Collected Documents*, ed. Donald Burrows, Helen Coffey, John Greenacombe and Anthony Hicks, 6 vols. (Cambridge: Cambridge University Press, 2013–), iv, 575–7.
2. This is not a book but a plan, measuring 6 and a half feet by 13 feet. For detailed information see *Handel: Collected Documents*, iv, 518–19.
3. Gainsborough's wife was the dedicatee of a 1729 edition and subscribed to another of 1731 (q.v.).
4. See above, pp. 13–14.
5. This publication was also subscribed to by Gainsborough's brother (James Noel), his cousin (Thomas Noel) and 'Captain Bennet Noël', presumably the Lieutenant General Bennett Noel (died 1766), to whose memory there is a monument by Nollekens in Exton parish church.
6. For Heighington's subscription list see Simon D. I. Fleming, 'The Musical Activities of the Spalding Gentlemen's Society', *Royal Musical Association Research Chronicle*, 48 (2017), 87–90.
7. Many of the 486 subscribers to this publication are listed in *Handel: Collected Documents*, iv, 445–6.

Appendix II
Documents on Music, Books and Theatre

The twenty-one documents in this Appendix form part of the collection of papers belonging to the Noel family of Exton Hall, Rutland, deposited in the Record Office for Leicestershire, Leicester and Rutland (ROLLR). All the documents in this collection are identified by the code DE3214, followed by an oblique stroke and a catalogue number (which may include a second oblique stroke).

The documents transcribed below are arranged in order of their catalogue number. Each is given a serial number to facilitate reference from the foregoing discussion. When a year appears in Old Style, the New-Style equivalent is supplied in square brackets, as are all other editorial additions. Most of the documents are bills. Monetary amounts are expressed in the British pre-decimal system, with twelve pence (d.) to the shilling and twenty shillings (s.) to the pound (£); the presentation of these amounts varies from document to document but is standardised in the transcriptions. At least one of the bills appears to have been wrongly totalled; the original, erroneous total is retained in the transcription, the correct amount given in the commentary. Each document is accompanied by a Commentary. When there are two or more comments in a single paragraph of a Commentary, they are separated by a pair of oblique strokes; cross-references from one document to another are given in parenthesis.

DOCUMENTS AND COMMENTARIES

1. DE3214/5575/3

Jan: 29: 1749/^{50} [1750]

Began Mich[aelmas]: 1748 and Ended Mich[aelmas]: 1749

	£	s.	d.
Order of L.^{d}: Gainsborough			
Kellem Berrey and his man 2 days setting up of sens		2	0
my self and my man 2 days taking them down		2	0
		4s.	0d.
Order of Mr Jackson			
Kell Berrey 18 days work att the Musick Rooms		18	0
my man 5 days att Same		5	0

66 *Appendix II*

Commentary

A bill for the erection and dismantling of scenery and for work on the music rooms, undertaken between Michaelmas (29 September) 1748 and Michaelmas 1749. This is the only known reference to music rooms at Exton. // Kellem (or Kell or Kenelm) Berrey, a carpenter, had worked at the Hall in July 1748 (see below, 15[a]1). Mr Jackson was identified as William Jackson in 1750 (16).

---

2. DE3214/5575/14

June 7th 1751

The Right. Hon.[ble] the Earl of Gainsborough
D[ebto]r To Saml Goodwin for Scene Painting &c.

	£	s.	d.
For Painting the New Stage for his Lordship's Account	5	5	0
The Model of the Stage	2	2	0
The Rock Scene in Athelwold	6	6	0
The Garden in D[o]	6	6	0
The Mountain Scene in the Double Falsehood	3	3	0
The Wood Scene D[o]	1	11	6
The Lodge D[o]		15	0
The Inn Yard for Harry y[e] 4th	1	1	0
The Stone in Jane Shore		5	0
The Bottom Part of y[e] Front of y[e] Stage		5	0
House Painting in the Lodging Room		10	6
1 white Woodcock		10	6
For Lodging at Geo. Hawleys	1	10	0
The Clouds		5	0
A Box and tape to measure with		5	0
	£30	0s.	6d.

[Received from the Countess on 26 November 1751]

Commentary

A bill from Samuel Goodwin, mainly for the painting of a stage and some scenery. When drafting the bill on 7 June 1751, Goodwin appears not to have known that Gainsborough had died on 21 March. // The new stage may have been the one mentioned in documents 15[b] and 16, which was built in 1750. // The plays mentioned in the bill are: *Athelwold* (by Aaron Hill); *Double Falsehood, or The Distressed Lovers* (Lewis Theobald) and *Jane Shore* (Nicholas Rowe); the 'Inn Yard' is the setting for Act II, scene

Appendix II 67

1, of Shakespeare's *Henry IV, Part I*. // That Goodwin painted scenery for these plays suggests that they were performed (see above, pp. 45–9). For further evidence on *Henry IV Part I* see below, 17[a] and 17[b]; for *Double Falsehood* see 18 and 19.

---

3. DE3214/5575/18

[Inside:]
　D[ebto]r to W[m] Lowe

1743		£	s.	d.
Nov[br] 23[d]	Repairing a Violin & Violincello & Varnishing the Same		5	0
1744				
24th Apr.	Repairing a Mahogona Stepl Ladder & a Sett of Castors for the Same		5	6
1746				
29th March	A Wallnut-tree Dressing table	1	1	0
		£1	11s.	6d.

[Outside:]
　M.[r] Lowe of Stamford his Bill [£]1 11s. 6d.
　Paid Dec.[r] 26 1751
　[Receipted 26 December 1751]

Commentary

A bill from William Lowe, a cabinet-maker in Stamford, Lincolnshire, for repairing a violin, a cello and a ladder, and presumably for supplying a dressing table. Although the bill was evidently submitted after Gainsborough's death in March 1751, the dates of Lowe's repairs are the earliest found in these documents.

---

4. DE3214/5575/22

A Bill from Ben: Christian

1749		£	s.	d.
Dec.[r] 26	A play bound and interleav'd		1	0
[1750]				
Jan: 4	Henry the fourth D[o]		1	0
15	Two Blanks for L.[d] Campden's use		6	0
	the Funeral bound and interleav'd		1	0
23	Hamlet bound			8
27	False Marriage bound and interleav'd		1	0

68 Appendix II

Feb: 3	Double Falsehood 8vo D^o	1	2
23	A Catalogue of Plays bound		8
Mar. 1	Fatal marriage D^o		8
13	Orphan D^o		6
1750			
30	King Lear 2 Vol.^{s} interleav'd	2	0
	Handel's Overtures 15 Vol^s at 1^s–3^d each	18	9
July 6	Writing a Vocal part in sampson for L:^{d} Campden	2	4½
31	Anthems 57 pages and aug.^{t} 6 D^o 40 pages	12	1½
Oct:^{r} 13	Hamlet bound		8
	Writing the Tragedy of Athelwold	12	6
Novr 8	Athelwold bound 2 Vol.^{s} Quarto	2	0
14	Hamlet interleav'd	1	0
Decr 10	Anthems Writing	1	6
11	Double Falsehood bound for L.^{y} Juliana		9
24	Jane Shore bound		8
[1751]			
Jan. 5	Double Falsehood interleav'd	1	2
	D^o bound		9
24	A Vol. of plays bound in Calf	1	6
		£3 11s.	5d.

[Receipted on 30 December 1751]

Commentary

A bill mainly for the binding and also for a little copying of plays and music. // The plays mentioned are: *Henry IV* (presumably Part 1: see above, 2); *The Funeral, or Grief a-la-mode* (Richard Steele); *Hamlet*; 'False Marriage'; *Double Falsehood* (see 2); *The Fatal Marriage, or The Innocent Adultery* (Thomas Southerne), for which incidental music had been composed by Henry Purcell (see Franklin B. Zimmerman, *Henry Purcell, 1659–1695: An Analytical Catalogue of his Music* (London: Macmillan, 1963), 270); *The Orphan, or The Unhappy Marriage* (Thomas Otway), *King Lear*, *Athelwold* and *Jane Shore* (see 2). // 'False Marriage' cannot be identified: the entry may refer to Aphra Behn's *The Forc'd Marriage*, or to Thomas Scott's *The Mock Marriage*, for which Purcell had composed three songs (Zimmerman, *Henry Purcell*, 280). // 'Lady Juliana' (11 December 1750), one of Gainsborough's daughters, is also mentioned in a bill for a dress (17[b]: 16 January 1751).

The first entry for music (30 March 1750) probably refers to the binding of the '60 printed ouvertures' that Christopher Smith had supplied in January (see 11). // The vocal part in 'sampson' was presumably used by Lord Campden, Gainsborough's ten-year-old son, in the performance of Handel's *Samson* in August 1750 (see 21). // The anthems (31 July and 10 December) cannot be identified: they may have included Handel's funeral anthem for

Queen Caroline (*The Ways of Zion do mourn*) and other pieces of 'proper Musick' performed in the chapel on 2 September 1750 (see 21).

5. DE3214/10185/196

[A single large sheet, with two columns of writing both on front and on back.]
The Right Hon.[ble] The Earl of Gainsborough to John Cooke Debtor

[Recto, column 1:]

		£	s.	d.
1748				
May 7	Rodericks Random 2 Vols.		6	0
	Voice of melody		4	6
	Essay on Dilacacy		2	6
14.th	Philips's Poems		2	0
	Livery Hats	3	16	6
	View of Clifden House		2	6
	View of Rotunda		2	6
	The Castle of Indolence		3	6
June 11th	L.[rd] Cam. M.[r] Noel & 2 Serv[ts] Hats	1	8	6
	Anson's Voyages Roy[ll] pap[r] b[ds]		5	0
21st	Ab: Bannier[s] Fables of Ant.[ts] 4 Vols.	1	4	0
	5 Sheets pastb.[rd] & blue paper		2	6
	Ansons Voyages 8.[vo] in ½ binding		5	0
July 1st	30 Q.[r] paper		19	6
	Life Q: Anne 2 Cov.[rs] & pastboard		3	0
Aug[st] 21st	His Lordship 1 Sup.[r] fine Hat		18	6
	wax		2	6
	6 Broad Folio paper books	1	10	0
21st	30 Q[r] Paper		19	6
Decem[r]	Gill Blass 4 Vols		7	6
9th	Moliers Plays 10 Vols.	1	10	0
	Memoirs of Woman of Pleasure		3	6
	Antidote Ag:[st] Melancolly		2	6
	Collect: of Songs. Lin.[t] Rob.[n] & Thrush 3 Vol.		6	0
	30 Q.[r] Paper Wax & Wafers	1	8	0
26th	Sherlock on Prophecy		4	6
	Ditto in French		4	6
[1749]				
Jan.[y] 2.[d]	2 Double Falshood 18[d] each		3	0
	Tryal of y[e] Witnesses		1	6
	Songs in y[e] Opera call'd Orazio		3	6
	French Vocabilary [sic]		3	6
	Lady[s] Religion		1	6
Jan.[y] 2.[d]	Paper & gilt paper & wax: 1		16	1
	4 Largest Testam.[ts] & Cas		12	0
	2 Common Prayers D.[o]		6	0
Feb 27	10 Q[r] best Dutch fools Cap		8	4
	Reason for giving up Gibraltar		1	6

Date	Item	£	s	d
March	Life of Augustus Cæsar 2 Vols.		6	0
	An Attempt to rescue Shakespear		1	6
7	Observa: on Man by Hartley 2 Vols		10	6
	L.r ab.t Exam: of two Brothers		1	0
	Advantages of Difin: Treaty			6
	2 Roman Hist: Q: & Answr		6	0
Mar: 21	Hist. of Tom Jones 6 Vols		18	0
1749	2 Gradus		5	0
	Lattin Bibles. Com: pray.r & Test. 3 Vol		10	6
April	1 Lattin Test: & 1 Com: prayr 2 V		5	0
17	Croffts Musica Sacra 3.d Vol	1	1	0
	Paper & Wax		19	6
	Universal History 20 Vols	5	0	0
	2 Vols Plays Ca: Lrd		2	6
	Tatlers 4 Vols		10	0
May	Atterburys Sermons 2 Vol		10	0
	Catalogue with prices & Car		2	6
17	Pindar by West 4to gilt		18	0
	4 Perspective Views		5	0
	L.r to a Lady		1	0
	4 Pamphlets		6	6
	Smiths Harmonicks		6	6
24th	Wittmills Kalendarium		2	6
	Mullers Attacks & defence Casd		6	6
	Rouchfts Maxims – – – Lrd		3	6
		£34	0s.	5d.

[Recto, column 2:]

Date	Item	£	s	d
1749	Songs in Jack ye Giant			6
	Frye Interest Great Britain		1	0
May	1 Broad Folio Paper book		4	6
24th	Danoil Maps of Italy colour'd		2	6
	Old Castles remarks		5	6
	Paruvian Lrs &c.		2	6
	Two Lrs from a Physitian		1	0
	Life of Betterton			6
	Millers Dict.y Fol 2 Vol	1	5	0
	Godwini de præsulibus 2. V L. P.		12	0
	1 D.o gilt b.d 2 Vols in one		14	6
29th	Livery Hats	4	4	0
	Pilkingtons Evang:1 Hist 1		18	0
	Popes L.rs L. P. gilt & Lrd		4	6
June	Drydens 6 Vols Lrd		1	6
5th	Correllos Solo.s Vestegan Dodwell & Com	1	17	6
	Sequel to the Tryal of Witnesses		1	6
	Hollingshead Chronicle 2 Vols.		3	3
	4.to Bible bound in Morrocco		14	6
July	6 Qr Largest 4to gilt paper		6	0
4th	Polite Arts		2	6
	Regicide		1	6
	Littleton Dictionary		8	6

	Stirlings Pantheon		1	6
	Stirlings Florus		3	6
15	Guthries Cicero 5 Vols	1	12	6
	Popes 4th & 5th Roy^ll pap^r cost	1	16	6
	Martins Virgil 2 Vol 4to	2	2	0
	Paper & Wax		16	6
	Tookes Pantheon		4	6
17	Anson Voyage L. P. b.^d silk & gilt		6	0
	10 Vols bound marble D°		12	6
	Popes Odd: 4to L. P. 5. Vols bound D°	1	10	0
	Salmon on Musick & Samaritan		3	6
	30 Q^r Paper		19	2
	Popes new Dunciad 4to gilt		4	6
	Martins Virgil 2 V bound D.°		10	6
	Rownings 3 Vols. Fitzosborne 2 Vols Trade 2 Vols & Miscell tracts 9 Vols		14	3
Aug^st 4th	10 Q^r Demy 4to Paper		8	4
	1 Skin of Parchm^t to Mr Chapman		1	6
	Hollingshead^s Chronicle 3^d V	1	15	0
	Whiston Life 2 Vols in boards		7	0
Sepr 13th	Magaz: N° 3. ye Governess. au^t of Liturgy		4	6
Octo^r 16	Pastboard & 10 Q^r to J. Mess		7	6
	Lady^s Religion		1	6
	Addyson^s Evidence^s JE" Relig:		3	0
	Life of Carew		2	6
	Amours of Zeokinizul		1	6
	Angola Histoire Indienne		3	0
	Stows Chronicles Folio		18	0
	Trip to the Jubilee		1	6
Novr 17	Wax & gilt paper		10	0
	Guardian^s 2 V 8° Roy.^ll paper		12	6
	1.st Vol only of Univer: Hist:		5	0
23^d	10 Q^r best cutt Dutch paper		8	4
	Clarissa 7 Vols	1	1	0
	Hist: Eng:^d Cutts & gilt		5	0
	Steele's Plays		2	6
		£35	9s.	7d.

[Verso, column 1:]

1749	1 Church Bible Folio Oxon		3	3	0
Decem.^r	7. Folio Vols musick Double=b^d silk & Double L^rd		2	12	0
28th	Royall Paper for musick			4	6
	Handels Songs & Venetian Ball 2 V Fol b^d			6	0
	10 Q^r Paper at 5^d a q^r			4	2
[1750]					
Jan 1	Guardian^s 2 Vol Royalle paper cost	1	1	0
	D° bound treblerola wth gold		5	0
	Sanby^s Horace 8.vo Edit: 2 Vols gilt		15	0
	New Method of Italian Tongue		6	0

72   Appendix II

Date	Item	£	s	d
	Free & Important Disquisition script		1	6
	State of Military Law		1	0
Feb 1	3 Almanacks		1	2
2.^{d}	Conquest of Mexico 2 Vol, & Condamines Voyage		13	6
16	20 Q^{rs} of Paper		14	6
	Chaplett musick		6	0
28th	Tasso Jerusalem		6	6
	Lobb on the Plague		6	6
	Court Register		2	6
1750	3 Q^r Fol Demy		6	0
	30 Q^r Paper & Wax	1	3	7
May	Latini Sermonis 5 Vols gilt		18	0
9th	Livery Hats	3	16	6
	2 Hughes Works 2 Vols at 6:^{s} 6		13	0
	Compleat Fisher			6
	Short on Tea &c:		6	0
	The Actor		3	6
27th	Herodian 6 6^d Maps of Geog: 6^s		12	6
	Universal pocket book		2	6
	Cannons of Criticisme		2	6
	Cibbers Life		6	6
	French Gramer &c		2	6
	2 Octavo Play^s interleav^d & b^d		3	0
	Paper for D^o		2	6
July 3^d	Folio Paper book ruld		4	6
5th	30 Q.^{r} of Paper		19	2
	Maps to Rollins History		4	6
	Antiq: of Windsor Roy^{ll} paper	1	1	0
	Compleat Angler		3	6
10.th	Views of Lrd Cobhams Gardens		4	0
	Dialogues on D.^{o} 18.^{d} wth Des[c]riptions		1	6
	Lenns Drawing Book		5	0
	2 Charact.^{r} of K.^{g} Char: 2^d at 3. 6		7	0
Sepr 6.	Paper		8	6
Octo^r 2.^{d}	30 Q^r of Paper	1	0	0
	Salmons Geography		6	6
2^d	Religion of Nature		6	6
	Description of Heraclea		3	0
	Lexicon Etymolog. Folio		15	0
5th	my Lords Hat		18	0
Octo^r	Travell^{rs} Pocket Compan:		1	6
12th	L'Esprit Du Loix 3 Vol gilt		13	6
	—— D^o in Eng^{sh} 2 Vols		12	6
	Lettres de Paschal		3	6
12th	6 Q.^{r} Demy		6	0
Novr 5.	6 Q^r D^o & wax 18.^{d}		7	6
	Heywood Fruitless Inquiry		2	6
	Folio musick Case & Lock clasp		4	6
	Stanyans Hist:^{y} of Greece 2 V gilt		12	0
	History of Greece Q: & Answer		3	6
		£31	3s.	7d.

[Verso, column 2:]

	2 Venice Preserv'd & interleav'd		3	6
1750	2 Child[s] Delight		2	0
	Lady[s] Memorand[um] book		1	0
Decem.[r] 10th	30 Q.[r] Paper		19	2
[1751]				
Jan.[y] 17.th	30 Q.[r] Ditto		19	2
	1 Pound of y[e] best wax		6	0
	2. Q[r] gold imbost paper		8	0
	Revolu: of Genoa 3 Vols		9	0
	Account of Madera		1	6
23[d]	œconomy of Human Life		2	0
	Musæ Anglicanæ 2 Vols		6	0
	Matair's Lucan out of print		3	6
	Clarks Ed: of Cæsars Com[y]		6	0
	Fletcher's Arithmetick		3	6
Feb 1	Salmons History 1.st Vol		5	0
	Græ. Grammat Eton:		2	0
5th	Cornel: Nepos: Oxon L. P.		5	0
	Merry Mans Companion		2	0
Mar: 2[d]	10 Q[r] Demy Paper		8	4
9th	295 N.[os] of Guthries Hist: at 6[d]	7	7	6
	Binding D[o] marb:[le] L.[rd] 3 Vols	1	4	0
	Swiffts Miscell: 13 V. marb[le]	2	2	0
March	12 Views of Rome		12	0
17th	6 Chinese Views		4	0
	Paper & wax		12	0
	Memoirs 2 Vols.		6	0
	3.[d] & 4.th Vols of Edwards on Painted Birds	4	4	0
	A View of Moon Light		4	0
	Bind[g] in Pastb[rds] Edward'[s] 2 Vols		4	0
	30 Q.[r] of paper		19	2
	Livery Hats	5	5	0
Dec[r] 1.st	Paper book omitted		5	0

£29	1s.	4d.
31	3	7
35	9	7
34	0	5
£129	14s.	11d.

Feb.y 15.th 1753 Reced of ~~the Rt Hon.ble~~ The Countess of Gainsborough Execut.x to The late R.t Hon.ble The Earl of Gainsborough the Contents in full p[er] John Cooke
From John Cooke Bookseller at Uppingham, Rutland.

[Cover sheet:]
M.r Cooke Book-Seller at Uppingham his Bill £129: 14: 11 /
Paid Feb.y y.e 15.th 1753
N°. 196

Commentary

This bill from John Cooke contains 212 entries, dated from 7 May 1748 to 17 March 1751, relating to the purchase of a large number of books (including a few on music), a large quantity of paper, a small amount of music, a number of prints and hats and other items. // Wafers were thin leaves of wax for sealing letters.

Books and Plays

Most of these are identified in the Index beginning on page 99 below, but a considerable number of the identifications are 'uncertain' and three items require comment. // The 'Life Q: Anne' (1 July 1748) cannot be identified, because at least eleven biographical accounts of the monarch were published between her death, in 1714, and 1748. // The entry 'Frye Interest Great Britain' (24 May 1749) probably refers to *The True and Real Interest of Great Britain Impartially Considered, with regard to the impending Rupture among the Northern Powers*, which is not attributed to an author in any known library catalogue: this bill may be unique in ascribing it to 'Frye'. // The 'Lady's Memorand[um] book' (5 November 1750) cannot be traced: the earliest known example of this kind of publication is *The Ladies Compleat Pocket-Book, for the Year of Our Lord, 1753*.

Music *(in the order mentioned in the document)*

'Voice of melody' (7 May 1748): the first edition of the first book of the *Voice of Melody* seems not to survive. *The Second Edition of the First Book [...] with Great Additions. The Anthems entirely New, and Great Part of the Psalm-Tunes Never before in Print, with some Choice Hymns* was 'collected, printed, and sold' by W[illiam] East of Waltham, Leicestershire, in 1750. In the same year East also published *The Second Book of the Voice of Melody, being a collection of the Most Curious Psalm-Tunes extant, in Four Parts; with variety of Hymns and Anthems; Likewise, M.r Hall's Te Deum and D.r Tudway's Magnificat: All in Score; Compos'd by the Most Eminent Masters for Four and Five Voices, as Sung in Cathedrals.*

'Antidote Ag:^st Melancolly' (9 December 1748) may have been a collection of music or a literary work or a mixture of both. A volume of ballads, songs and catches had been published under that title in 1661 and, as *Wit and Mirth. An Antidote against Melancholy*, in 1682. The title was revived in the mid-eighteenth century for *An Antidote against Melancholy. Being a collection of Fourscore Merry Songs […] the Music of them all entirely New*, which appeared in 1749, possibly too late for inclusion in this bill. Meanwhile, the title had also been used for a collection of prose, verse and songs – *Laugh and Be Fat, or, An Antidote against Melancholy. Containing […] Intrigues and Stories […] Poems on Various Occasions […] Pleasant Songs and Ballads* – of which the twelfth edition had been published in 1741.

'Collect: of Songs. Lin.^t Rob.^n & Thrush 3 Vol.' (9 December 1748) is a reference to *Orpheus: A collection of One Thousand Nine Hundred Seventy Four […] English and Scotch Songs. Vol. 1: The Linnet; vol. 2: The Robin; vol. 3: The Thrush* (London: C. Hitch and J. Osborn, 1749).

'Songs in ye Opera call'd Orazio' (2 January 1749): the pasticcio *Orazio* was first seen in London on 29 November 1748, and Walsh's edition of *The Favourite Songs in the Opera call'd Orazio* was published before the end of the year (see *George Frideric Handel: Collected Documents*, ed. Donald Burrows, Helen Coffey, John Greenacombe and Anthony Hicks, 6 vols. (Cambridge: Cambridge University Press, 2013–), iv, 611 and 618).

William Croft's *Musica Sacra, or Select Anthems in Score* had been published in two volumes [1724, 1725], so the meaning of '3.^d Vol' in this bill (17 April 1749) is unclear.

'Songs in Jack ye Giant' (24 May 1749) probably refers to Henry Brooke's *The Songs in Jack the Gyant Queller. An Antique History*, of which the second edition (1749) provides the words of the airs but not the tunes.

'Corrello^s Solo.^s' (5 June 1749) must be an edition of Corelli's sonatas for violin and continuo, op. 5, first published in Rome (1700). This entry could refer to Walsh's edition – *XII Solos for a Violin with a Thorough Bass for the Harpsicord or Violoncello* [1740] – or to the *Sonate a Violino e Violono o Cimbalo* published by Benjamin Cooke in c. 1735 (cf. Hans Joachim Marx, *Die Überlieferung der Werke Arcangelo Corellis: Catalogue raisonnée* (Cologne: Arno Volk-Hans Gerig, 1980), 181–2).

'Handels Songs' (28 December 1749) probably refers to volume 1 of *Handel's Songs selected from his latest Oratorios for the Harpsicord, Voice, Hoboy or German Flute*, published by Walsh in 1748 (see William C. Smith and Charles Humphries, *Handel: A Descriptive Catalogue of the Early Editions*, 2nd edn (Oxford: Blackwell, 1970), 190–91; *Handel: Collected Documents*, iv, 616–17); alternatively, the entry could denote some of the volumes of *Apollo's Feast* that Walsh had published between 1725 and 1740 (Smith and Humphries, *Handel*, 161–4; *Handel: Collected Documents*, ii, 9; iii, 524, 649 and 652).

76 *Appendix II*

'Venetian Ball' (28 December 1749) is a reference to the *Venetian Ballads* of Johann Adolf Hasse 'and all the Celebrated Italian Masters', published by Walsh between 1742 and 1750 (William C. Smith and Charles Humphries, *A Bibliography of the Musical Works Published by the Firm of John Walsh during the Years 1726–1766* (London: The Bibliographical Society, 1968), 186–7).

William Boyce's 'Chaplett musick' (16 February 1750) was published in 1750 as *The Chaplet. A Musical Entertainment. As it is perform'd at the Theatre-Royal in Drury-Lane*.

'Merry Mans Companion' (5 February 1751) is a collection of songs – *The Merry Man's Companion and Evening's Agreeable Entertainer, containing near Six Hundred* [...] *Songs, Catches, Airs, &c.* [...] *Together with the Songs of the Late Seasons at the Public Gardens* (London: H. Kent and Thomas Payne, 1750).

Prints

The 'views' of 'Clifden House' and the Rotunda (14 May 1748) were probably prints of Cliveden House, Taplow (Berkshire), which was built in 1666 by the 2nd Duke of Buckingham, and of the Rotunda at Ranelagh Gardens, Chelsea; these Gardens were opened to the public in 1742. // The entry 'Views' of Lrd Cobham's Gardens' (10 July 1750) doubtless refers to the gardens of Richard Temple, 1st Viscount Cobham, at Stowe, Buckinghamshire, where 'Capability' Brown was head gardener in the 1740s. // The '12 Views of Rome' (9 March 1751) may have been by Gian Paolo Panini (1691–1765), the most popular eighteenth-century painter of views of Rome. Prints of his works circulated widely, and according to Jenny Clark, 'Exton and the Noel Family', *Rutland Record*, 19 (1999), 384, Gainsborough acquired some of them. // It has not been possible to identify the other views mentioned in the document.

6. DE3214/10185/201

[Inside:]
The Right Hon:^{ble} the Countess of Gainsborough's
Bill due to George Wright

	£	s.	d.
For Instructing ye Ladys on ye Harpsicord from ye Twenty first of July 1750 to ye first Week in Octo^{br} 1750. Eleven Weeks at ye Rates of one Pound one Shill.^{g} Per Week	11	11	0
Two Weeks after ye Above Account by his Lordship's order	2	2	0
For Strings and Repairs for ye Harpsicords		10	6
	£14	3s.	6d.

[Reverse: receipt in the hand of George Wright:]
    May y.^{e} 3.^{d} 1753
    Rec.^{d} of the Executer of the Right Hon:^{le} the Earl of Gainsborough
    the full Contents of this Bill and In full of all Demands
    by me George Wright

[Outside:]
    (N.º 201)
    Mr Wright,
    Musick Master
    £14 3s. 6d.
    _____

    Paid May ^{ye} 3.^{d}
    1753

Commentary

A bill from George Wright for giving the 'Ladys' harpsichord lessons from July to October 1750 and for repairing the instruments. // The 'Ladys' were Gainsborough's daughters – presumably Jane and Juliana, who had sung in *Comus* in 1748, and possibly Elisabeth, who had taken the role of the Lady. // Wright cannot be securely identified, but a 'Mr George Wright of Hereford' had subscribed to William Hayes, *Twelve Arietts or Ballads and Two Cantatas* (1735), and a 'Mr George Wright' to Henry Carey, *The Musical Century in One Hundred English Ballads* [...] *Vol. 1. Containing the First Fifty*, 2nd edn (1740). // Nothing more is known about Wright's employment as music master at Exton – neither how long it lasted nor whether it was regular or occasional. He may not have been the music master expected by Gainsborough in 1745 to make a copy of Handel's finale to *Comus* (see Betty Matthews, 'Unpublished Letters concerning Handel', *Music & Letters*, 40 (1959), 265; *Handel: Collected Documents*, iv, 323; Colin Timms, 'Handel and *Comus* at Exton', in *New Perspectives on Handel's Music: Essays in Honour of Donald Burrows*, ed. David Vickers (Woodbridge: Boydell, 2022), 252–4).

---

7. DE3214/10186/6

[Front:]

    Stamford   Bought of Andrew Rogers

		£	s.	d.
1748				
7 April.	To Robinson Corisoe 2 Vol.^{s}		5	0
	Classical Dictionary. 2 Vol.^{s}		6	0
11.	a Broad Folio 6 Quires fools. Cap. Rul'd		6	6
15.	Binding Handell's Joshua 1:st part 4:^{to}		3	0
	The 7 First Numbers of Albinus's Anatomical Prints. — at 2^s/6^d		17	6

78 Appendix II

Date	Item	£	s	d
28.	Binding Handell's Joshua 2:^{d} part		3	0
8 May	Binding. — ditto 3:^{d} part —		3	0
16. June	The Case of Mon:^{r} Bourdonnais			6
	History of Character of St. Paul Exam.^{d}		2	0
	First Book of Ovid's Art of Love paraphras'd		2	0
	Apology for a Late Resignation		1	0
	Print of S:^{r} Peter Warren		1	6
	—— The Same of Lord Anson		1	6
	The Gallant Companion		3	0
	2. Copies of Anson's Voyage — 8.vo		12	0
— 20.	1. Quire of Cartridge Paper		1	0
8 July	Binding Israel in Egypt Royal Folio		7	6
— 20.	½ Quire of Cartridge Paper			6
12. Aug.^{t}	½ Binding a Quire of Royal 4.to Musick		2	0
16.	The Fair penitent			6
2. Sep:^{r}	½ Binding 4 Vol:^{s} of Royal 4.to Musick		8	0
9.	— ditto & interleaving Othello.			9
— 10.	4 Copys of Edward & Eleonora. at 1/6		6	0
	4 —— Drummer at 6.^{d}		2	0
	4. King Lear		2	0
	4. Rich.^{d} 3.^{d}		2	0
	2. Walking Statue		1	0
	1 Cobler of Preston.			6
	1 Dryden's Plays 6 Volumes.		18	0
27	½ binding & Interleaving Othello 8:^{vo}		1	0
2:^{d} Octob:^{r}	1. Othello in 12:^{mo} & ½ bind:^{g} & Interleaving it		1	3
11	2. Quires of Cartridge Paper		2	0
14	½ binding & Interleaving the Drummer			9
2:^{d} Nov:^{r}	½ Binding 2:^{d} part of Henry 4th: 6 1. Henry 4:th 2: part & to ½ Binding & Interleaving it		1	3
[1749]				
3: March.	Sewing Fitz: Osborne's Letters 8:^{vo} boards			4
	½ Binding a Quarto Volume of Manuscript Musick. — (not Letter'd)		1	8
21:st	4 Quires of Cartridge Paper		4	0

[Back:]

1749

Date	Item	£	s	d
7. April	To ½ binding 11 Musick Books Royal 4:^{to} of different Sizes (as to thickness &c.^{a}) at 1^s/6^d one with another.		16	6
1750	4. Cobler of Preston		2	0
6 May.	Merry Wives of Windsor			6
	½ binding & Interleaving it			9
21:st June	Binding the Sopha 2 Voll. in 1 Tome 12.mo calf Letter'd		1	0
14 July.	Du Pin's Life of Christ 8:^{vo}		2	6
	Congreve's Works 3 Volumes 8:^{vo}		9	0
	Croxalls Fables		3	0
	Sent this Acc.^{t} to L:^{d} Gainsbro'	£8	7s.	3d.

1750			
22 august	Binding Sampson an Oratorio 3 Vol:^{s} 4.to	12	0
14 Sept:^{r}	½ Binding the Report of the proceedings of the Board of General Affairs concerning Cope, Lascelles, [Fowke] 4:^{to}	2	0
26. Oct:^{r}	½ Binding & Interleaving Athelrode a Play		9
6 Nov.^{r}	6 Sheets of Imboss'd Paper	1	0
12 Dec.^{r}	Venice preserv'd ½ bound & interleav'd	1	3
27	Jane Shore —— ditto ——	1	3
	1 ditto ½ bound only	1	0
[1751]			
11. Jan.^{y}	½ binding & interleaving Henry 4:th 1:st p.^{t} 8:^{vo}	1	0
	—— the Same 2:^{d} part — d.^{o}	1	0
	½ binding Double discovery 8:^{vo}		9
6. Febr:^{y}	Binding the œconomy of Hum:^{n} calf Gilt	1	3
	Altering the Binding of the 3.^{d} Vol; of Shakespeare — 8.vo		6
1751			
1.st March.	The Musæum	1	0
	Comic Tunes in Queen Mab	1	6
	A Life of Owen Tudor	2	0
	Adventures of Wm Willes	1	0
	Thoughts on the present Game Laws		6
	Total	£9 17s.	0d.

[Receipted by Andrew Rogers on 17 February 1752]

[Cover sheet:]
    1752. Mr And.^{w} Rogers.
    Stacioner Bill.
    £ s. d.
    9 17 0
    Paid the full Contents of all
    Demand to 17 Feb.^{r} 1752

Commentary

A bill from Andrew Rogers of Stamford for the purchase and binding of books, plays and music and the purchase of paper. // The majority of the books and plays can be identified, but two are 'uncertain': 'Du Pin's Life of Christ' (14 July 1749) and 'The Musæum' (1 March 1751). // Daniel Defoe's novel *Robinson Crusoe* (7 April 1748) was first published in 1717 and adapted as a pantomime later in the century (see Sybil Rosenfeld, *Temples of Thespis: Some Private Theatres and Theatricals in England and Wales, 1700–1820* (London: Society for Theatre Research, 1978), 26). // Nicholas Rowe's *The Fair Penitent* (16 August 1748) was first performed in 1703, with music by John Eccles, and became very popular with amateur performers (Rosenfeld, *Temples of*

80 *Appendix II*

Thespis, 169). // *The Cobbler of Preston* is the title of two plays dating from 1716, one by Christopher Bullock, the other by Charles Johnson; that the title appears twice in this bill (on 10 September 1748 and 6 May 1750) suggests that Gainsborough bought both. // Samuel Croxall's *Fables of Æsop* (14 July 1749), first published in 1722, went through fifteen editions by 1790 (see John Brewer, *The Pleasures of the Imagination: English Culture in the Eighteenth Century* (Abingdon: Routledge, 2013), 364). // 'Double Discovery' (11 January 1751) refers to Dryden's *The Spanish Fryar, or, The Double Discovery* (1681), for which Purcell composed a song in 1695 (Zimmerman, *Henry Purcell*, 288–9).

Most of the entries for music refer to binding, not purchase. In addition to much unidentified music, three oratorios by Handel were bound – *Joshua* (15 April, 28 April and 8 May 1748), *Israel in Egypt* (8 July) and *Samson* (22 August 1750). *Joshua* was first performed on 9 March 1748, so Gainsborough must have moved quickly to acquire a manuscript copy. // Only one musical item appears to have been purchased (on 1 March 1751): *The Comic Tunes in Queen Mab. As they are perform'd at the Theatre Royal Drury Lane. Set for the Violin, German Flute or Hoboy, with a Thorough Bass for the Harpsicord; Composed by the Society of the Temple of Apollo* were published by James Oswald in 1751 (Edith B. Schnapper, *The British Union-Catalogue of Early Music printed before the Year 1801*, 2 vols. (London: Butterworths Scientific Publications, 1957), ii, 868).

The prints of Sir Peter Warren and Lord Anson (16 June 1748) suggest that Gainsborough was interested in maritime affairs. Peter Warren (1703/4–52) was a distinguished naval officer and politician whose portrait was painted by Thomas Hudson in 1751. George Anson (1697–1762), 1st Baron Anson, sailed round the world in 1740–44 and became First Lord of the Admiralty; Gainsborough purchased three copies of the account of his voyage (document 5, 11 June 1748; document 7, 16 June).

8. DE3214/10186/12

A Bill for the Right Hon.[ble] the Countis of Gainsborough
    from Anthony Herring

	£	s.	d.
For 25 Days Works helping to Build the Stage in the Hall	1	5	0
My Prentice 20 Days at 6:[d] p[er] Day		10	0

[Receipted on 20 January 1752]

Commentary

Since Anthony Herring, a carpenter, addressed his bill to the countess, it must date from after her husband's death in March 1751. His work is undated, but the stage he helped build may be the one mentioned in documents 2, 15[b] and 16, which appears to have been constructed in 1750.

9. DE3214/10186/16

Bill from Francis Sharp for bell-ringing on 18 May, 29 June, 13 August, 18 September, 22 November and 17 March 1750/[51].

[At the end:]

	£	s.	d.
For Concert playing			
Feb.[y] the 4.th and 7.th [1751]		10	0
Michael & John Sharp one day		10	0

[Reverse:]
Allow.d. 4: 6: 9 W Blathwayt / Jan.[y] 13.th 1752
Rec.[d] the Contents of this bill in Full of all Demands by the Hands of W Blathwayt £4: 6: 9 Francis Sharp

Commentary

The bell-ringing presumably took place in the church of St Peter and St Paul, now Exton parish church. The dates from May to November were in 1750, but 17 March was in 1751, four days before Gainsborough's death. // Nothing is known about the two concerts, except that the rate of pay must have been five shillings a day, with Francis playing on both 4 and 7 February 1751, and Michael and John on one day each. The bill does not identify the instruments or the music that they played. // These musicians do not appear to have been related to those depicted in Johann Zoffany's painting of the Sharp family who from 1753 held music parties on the River Thames (for secondary literature on the Sharps and Zoffany, see Chapter 2, note 30). // At Exton a 'Tho. Sharp' was paid six guineas in 1756 and a Will Sharp £1 12s. 6d. in 1765 ('List of Servants 1751–1772': ROLLR, DE3214/8528).

10. DE3214/10187/11

M.[r] W.[m] Shropshire / Stationers Bill

		£	s.	d.
1748 [1749]	To Two Royal African		2	0
Mar 8	The Print of the Fire Works		1	0
	Aglionby's Lives of The Painters		8	0
	Nature Display'd 4 Vol: Cutts		12	0
	Seed's Sermons 2 Vol:		10	0
	A Dialogue T. Jones and J. Smith			6

Appendix II

Date	Item	£	s	d
17	Solomon an Oratorio		1	0
	Binding 2:d Vol: of Fitzosborne ½ Bind			6
20	The Spectators 16 Vol: Bound in Calf Extr and: Marble'd Leaves	3	0	0
	The first and 2:d Part Fitzosborne Letters		7	0
	2:d Vol: Ditto		3	6
	Du Bos on Poetry Painting &c 3 Vol: Lett.d		15	0
	2 Setts of Littleton's Sermons 2 Vol: in 12.mo Lett.d		12	6
	Hartley's Book 2 Vol: Oct° ½ Binding		9	0
23	Two Messiahs An Oratorio		2	0
	Pope's Odyssey 5 Vol: in Boards		11	0
26	Essay on Design		1	6
	Tom Jones 6 Vol: in Boards		16	0
Ap:l 21:st 1749	Merope a new play		1	6
May 22	Essay on Air on Bodies 2 Vol: Calf Extr:		13	6
	Life of Homer Ditto Bind: Extr.		6	9
	Letters Concerning Mythology Ditto		6	9
	Lord Bolingbrooke's Letters		3	6
June 3	2 Vol: of Edwards on Birds Coulour'd		2	2
21	Theobald's Shakespear 7 Vol: Oct:° g.d & Lett:d	2	2	0
Dec 6	Paid 2:d Subscription to Newton's Milton		10	6
	Doing up Ditto 2 Vol. Quarto		3	6
[1750]				
Jan 23	Paid Carriage for Ditto by York Coach		2	6
Feb 10	Pozzo's Perspective folio Cutts	1	5	0
	2 Fatal Marriage		1	0
	Paid the Carriage by York Coach		2	6
		£16	13s.	6d.

Rec:d Jan.y 13:th 1752 by the hands of Benjamin Andrews the contents of this Bill and in full of all claims and demands whatever on the Estate of the late Earl of Gainsborough
[autograph signature] W:m Shropshire

Commentary

A bill mainly for the purchase of books. Most of them are identified in the Index below (p. 99ff), but the identity of the following is uncertain: 'Two Royal African' and 'Nature Display'd' (both 8 March 1749), 'Littleton's Sermons' (20 March) and 'Life of Homer' (22 May). // The subscription to 'Newton's Milton' (6 December 1749) was presumably the subscription to Thomas Newton's edition of *Paradise Lost* (1749), listed in Appendix I. // To judge by the prices, the entries 'Solomon' (17 March 1749) and 'Two Messiahs' (23 March) refer to printed wordbooks of Handel's oratorios. The dates of purchase coincide with the first performance of *Solomon* and a revival of *Messiah*, both at Covent Garden (*Handel: Collected Documents*, iv, 649–50, 657–8): these wordbooks must therefore have been bought in London. // Benjamin Andrews may have assisted in the administration of Gainsborough's estate: his name appears in a similar context in documents 11, 13 and 14. A servant named 'Ann Andrews' was paid £3 10s. 0d. at Exton in 1765 ('List of Servants 1751–1772': ROLLR DE3214/8528).

The 'Print of the Fire Works' (8 March 1749) was an engraving of the structure for the display in Green Park for which Handel composed his celebrated *Music for the Royal Fireworks*. The performance took place on 27 April, but prints of the planned structure had been available for purchase since the end of 1748 (*Handel: Collected Documents*, iv, 619–21 and 687–9).

11. DE3214/10187/18

M.r Smith M.r Handels wrighter
 The Right Hon.ble Earl of Gainsborough
 M.r Blathwayt Knows of These

		£	s.	d.
Jan: 3.d 1749. [1750]	60 printed ouvertures	3	3	0
	Carrige & Porter		3	6
August 11: 1750,	a Set of M.r Handels new Concerto's	1	1	0
	Ditto old once		12	0
	Corelli's D.o		15	0
	5 Books of Opera Dances at 6.s	1	10	0
	Carritge & porter		2	6
August 17.	12 printed Books of Sampson		12	0
	Carrige		2	0
Sep.r 18.th	a Song in Demetrius		3	0
22.d	D.o 4 Songs		6	6
	porter &		1	0
	part of a Chorus in Sampson		2	6
	payd the Carrige of the Oratorio of Sampson		2	6
		£8	16s.	6d.
				Rt.

Rec.d Jany 25th, 1752 the contents of this Bill & in full of all
 claims & demands whatever on the Estate of the late Earl
 of Gainsborough. by the hands of Benj: Andrews
 [autograph signature] Christopher Smith

Commentary

A bill from Christopher Smith, Handel's copyist and manager, for the supply and delivery of music and librettos. The original was reproduced in miniature

84 *Appendix II*

in Jenny Clark, 'Family Annals: The Exton Manuscripts', *Rutland Record*, 13 (1993), 121. The entries can be identified as follows.

'60 printed ouvertures': Walsh's edition of the orchestral parts of the overtures to all of Handel's operas and oratorios (see *Handel: Collected Documents*, iv, 759). // 'Handels new Concerto's': presumably his *Twelve Grand Concertos*, op. 6 (*c.* 1740–41), which were reprinted in 1746 (Smith and Humphries, *Handel*, 222–3). // 'Ditto old once' [i.e., ones]: presumably Handel's *Concerti Grossi*, op. 3 (1734), which were reprinted in the 1740s (Smith and Humphries, *Handel*, 218–20). // Corelli's D.º: the *Concerti Grossi*, op. 6, of Arcangelo Corelli. This edition cannot be securely identified. The instrumental parts of Corelli's *Concerti Grossi con duoi violini e violoncello di concertino obligati* had been issued by Walsh in *c.* 1730 and reissued in *c.* 1740, 1745 and 1749; *The Score of the Twelve Concertos* appeared in 1735 and again in 1740 (Smith and Humphries, *A Bibliography*, 91–3).

'5 Books of Opera Dances': presumably the five books of *Comic Tunes to* [...] *Opera Dances*, published by Walsh between 1741 and 1747 (Smith and Humphries, *A Bibliography*, 176–8, nos. 786–90). // '12 printed Books of Sampson': costing a shilling apiece, these clearly were wordbooks of Handel's *Samson*. // 'Song in Demetrius', an opera by Giovanni Battista Pescetti: this could have been *'The Charmer'* [...] *To a Celebrated Air in Demetrius* [*c.* 1740] or *'Semplicetta tortorella'*. Sung by Sig^{ra} Francesina [Elisabeth Duparc] in *Demetrius* [London, *c.* 1737] (cf. Schnapper, *The British Union-Catalogue*, i, 264). // 'D.º 4 Songs' could relate to *The Favourite Songs in the Opera call'd Demetrius* (London: Walsh, [1737]), which, however, contains seven songs (Schnapper, *The British Union-Catalogue*, ii, 775). Contemporary collections comprising four songs (not related to *Demetrius*) include *Four New and Diverting Songs performed at the Theatres and Publick Entertainments* (London: Walsh and Hare, [1728]) (Smith and Humphries, *A Bibliography*, 312–13) and *Four Favourite Songs sung by Mr Beard at Ranelagh Gardens* (London: J. Johnson, [*c.* 1750]) (Schnapper, *The British Union-Catalogue*, ii, 965). // The penultimate entry – 'part of a Chorus in Sampson' – must have been a manuscript copy, prepared by Smith or one of his assistants

---

12. DE3214/10187/19

[Inside:]		£	s.	d.
Sepr 5	To 20 Rings of first Strings for a Violin		10	0
1748	For 2 Silver thirds for a Tennour		2	0
	To 4 Silver thirds for a Violoncello		4	0
Decem.^{r} 2^d	To 2 fourths di^{to}		5	0
	To 2 Quire of Royal paper		6	0

[1749]				
July [recte January]	To Strings for a Bass and Tennor		10	6
y[e] 18th	Payd Carridge		2	6
March y[e] 11th	For two Royal Books		10	0
24th	To a Sett of Small Strings for a Little Base		3	0
	To a Screw Bow	1	1	0
May y[e] 5th	To putting a Double Base in order and a new Bow	3	3	0
	Payd for a Packing Case		14	0
	For a Bow without a Screw		15	0
		£8	10s.	6d.

I had an order from A Gentleman to Send Down a Bill of what Claims
I had on the Late Right Hon.[ble] Earl of Gainsborough, which is exactly
stated from my Books in the above Bill.
May y[e] 20[th] 1751 I am S.[r] your most Humble Serv[t]
Al[i]ce Walmsly.

[Outside:]
M.[rs] Al[i]ce Walmsly for
Violing Strings &c.

£   s.   d.
8   10   6

[Receipted by Alice Walmsly on 23 January 1752]

Commentary

Mrs Walmsly may have been related to Peter Wamsley, Walmsley or Warmsley, a maker of violins, violas and cellos who was active in London in about 1725–45 (cf. *The New Grove Dictionary of Music and Musicians,* 2nd edn (London: Macmillan, 2001), *s.v.* Wamsley). // Her bill was added up incorrectly: the total should be £8 6s. 0d. Nevertheless, she was paid in full.

Mrs Walmsly's bill for goods and services relating to stringed instruments should be considered in conjunction with that from Michael Christian Festing (13), and both of these bills could usefully be compared with the list of Felice Giardini's expenditure at the Simpson/Cox music shop from July 1751 to February 1758 (see Cheryll Duncan, *Felice Giardini and Professional Music Culture in Mid-Eighteenth-Century London* (Royal Musical Association Monographs 35) (Abingdon: Routledge, 2020), Chapter 5 and Appendix 1.

According to Duncan, *Felice Giardini*, 80, a 'ring' was probably a coiled string; Mrs Walmsly's charge of 10s. for '20 Rings of first Strings for a Violin' equates to 6d. per E string, the price paid by Giardini in the early 1750s. // Silver strings were gut strings wound with silver wire. // The word

86   *Appendix II*

'tennor' or 'tennour' probably denotes a viola. // The charge of 6s. for two quires of Royal paper compares favourably with the 16s. for four quires, paid by Giardini on 18 March 1752 (Duncan, *Felice Giardini*, 103). // The 'Little Base' was probably a small double bass, possibly intended for a child. // The references to bows with and without a screw are noteworthy. The screw-adjustable frog and eyelet had been developed in about 1700 and come to England in around 1740, but bows with a traditional clip-in frog continued to be made and used long after that: see John Dilworth, 'The Violin and Bow – Origins and Development', in *The Cambridge Companion to the Violin*, ed. Robin Stowell (Cambridge: Cambridge University Press, 2011), 1–29, at 24–5, and *The New Grove Dictionary*, s.v. Bow, §I, 3: c. 1625–c. 1800.

13. DE3214/10187/26

Ld Gainsborough		£	s.	d.
Nov:[br] 10. 1747	Strings, Bridges, and Pins for A Violin, exclusive of 10 strings return'd		18	0
Dec:[br] 2.	A Violoncello Bow	1	2	0
	A Violin Bow		15	0
	Paid for Twisting of Handles with Catlings		2	0
	A Box to send them in		1	0
	Carriage paid for ye Bows		2	6
	A Porter			6
[1748]				
Jany 6. 1747/^{8}.	A Violoncello Bow	1	2	0
	Twisting of Handles with Catling		1	0
	A Box to send it in		1	0
	Carriage Paid		2	6
	Porter			6
		£4	8s.	0d.

[Overleaf:]
Rec Jany 23, 1752 by the hands of Benj: Andrews the contents of this Bill and in full of all claims & demands on the Estate of the late Earl of Gainsborough,
p[ro] Mic: Festing

Commentary

A bill from the composer and violinist Michael Christian Festing (1705–52) for goods and services relating to stringed instruments, an aspect of his activities hitherto unknown. // Arising from the period between 10 November 1747 and 6 January 1748, this bill precedes that of Mrs Walmsly (12), which refers to the period from 5 September 1748 to 5 May 1749. // A catling (or catline) string was made by twisting two or more gut strings together: see Djilda Abbot and Ephraim Segerman, 'Gut strings', *Early Music*, 4 (1976), 430–37, at 431. Festing's bill suggests that a catling could be used to make or improve the handle of a bow. // Both Gainsborough and his wife had subscribed (independently) to Festing's *Twelve Sonata's in Three Parts*, op. 2 (1731), and the countess had also been a subscriber to his *Twelve Solo's for a Violin and Thorough Bass*, op. 1 (1730): see above, Appendix I. // Taken together, these subscriptions and this bill suggest that Festing was known personally to Gainsborough and his wife.

14. DE3214/10187/38

[Autograph letter and bill from Louis-François Roubiliac]

[f. 1r:] London the 20 May 1751
A person Came to me friday last to tel me from you, to send a frash bill for my demands upon Lord Gainsborough, for there was a Busto of Pope never reciev'd, whan I send the seaid Bustos I send lickewise a bil to his Lordship, but as it is 4. yeare past it has slipt my memory and were lickly have mistook names [f. 1v:] but I have shure that that [*sic*] there was 3. sent. down, therfor as I supose the are existing yet, you may know, better than I what the are, for My Lord gave me to understand that the ware to stand all ~~togerthe~~ tagethar an so you'l be so good as to fill up the name in the bill I am S.^{r}

Your mos humble / and obediant Servant
L. F. Roubiliac

I hop my being a foriner wil bee an apologie for ~~an~~ faults in stile or spelling

						£	s.	d.
[f. 2r:] A Busto of Sr Isaac Newton in plaister						2	2	0
1 d.º	"					~~2~~	~~2~~	~~0~~
1 d.º of Handle	"					3	3	0
3 pakin Cases						1	2	6
	£	s	d			£8	9s.	6d.
Popes Head not Reced	2.	2.	0)					
third part of Packing Case		7.	6)	Deduct		2	9	6
				Remains		£6	0s.	0d.

Received 21 February 1752 by the hands of Benjamin Andrews.
 [Autograph signature of Roubiliac]

Appendix II

Commentary

The French sculptor Louis-François Roubiliac (1702–62), who created the famous statue of Handel for Vauxhall Gardens (now in the Victoria and Albert Museum) and the Handel monument in Westminster Abbey, also made busts of the composer for prominent patrons. // This letter reveals that Roubiliac had been commissioned by Gainsborough to supply busts of Handel, Isaac Newton and Alexander Pope, presumably for his residence at Exton, and that the bust of Pope had not arrived. It is not known whether the busts of Newton and Handel are preserved at Exton or whether that of Pope resides elsewhere. // Two or three guineas for a plaster bust by Roubiliac appears to have been a relatively modest price: his terracotta bust of the castrato Francesco Bernardi ('Senesino'), dating probably from 1735, is said by the singer to have cost £7 15s. (Malcolm Baker, 'Sculpting Reputation: A Terracotta Bust of Senesino by Roubiliac', *Metropolitan Museum Journal*, 57 (2022), 25–40, at 27), while those of Lady Grisel Baillie and Lady Murray each cost ten guineas in 1745 (Baker, *The Marble Index: Roubiliac and Sculptural Portraiture in Eighteenth-Century Britain* (New Haven: Yale University Press, 2014), 292). // For further discussion of the present document see Colin Timms, 'Lord Gainsborough buys a Bust of Handel from Roubiliac', *Händel-Jahrbuch*, 67 (2021), 59–71. For Handel and Roubiliac in general see David Hunter, *The Lives of George Frideric Handel* (Woodbridge: Boydell, 2015), 368–85, and Hans Joachim Marx, *'By Heaven Inspired': Die Bildnisse von Georg Friedrich Händel* (Lilienthal: Laaber, 2021), 61–109.

---

15. DE3214/10188/104

[a] N.º 2 Noum^e 1: 1748
A Bill For the Right Honble Earle of Gainsborough from Jo.^{n} Fancort

			£	s.	d.
1: July 13 1748	John Fancort 17 days Setting up the Scens in the Gardin and taking down and other work a bout them			17	0
	John Hobs 16 Days att Same			16	0
	Will Fancort 12 days			6	0
	Phill Gann 11 days			11	0
	Antony Herring's man 5 days			5	0
	Tho Chapman 2 days			2	0
	Kell berrey 16 days and his man 16 days		1	12	0
			£4	9s.	0d.
2:	John Fancort 4 days Setting up the Scens in the hall the first time			4	0
	John Hobs 4 days att Same			4	0
	Will Fancort 4 days att Same			2	0
	Kell berrey 2 days and his man 2 days same			4	0
				14s.	0d.

Appendix II 89

3:	John Fancort 16 days Setting up the Scens in the hall the Last time and making other new things about them		16	0
	John Hobs 1 day att Same		1	0
	Will Fancort 11 days att Same		5	6
	Kell berrey 16 days and his man 6 days	1	2	0
		£2	4s.	6d.
	In all	£7	7s.	6d.

Aug.st 11: 1751
Reced the full Contents of this Bill
for me [autograph signature:] John Fan Carubet [?]

[b] A Bill For y.e Right Honble Earl of Gainsborough
Began Septem 1749 and Ended December 1750

Order of Ld Gainsborough		£	s.	d.
John Fancourt	29 Days making of a Book-at 18 a Day-kess in m.r Skiners rome and Repairing ye wainscot	2	3	6
John Hobs	4 Days att Same		4	0
John Fancourt	33 Days Setting up Senes in ye hall and Repairing of Them	2	9	6
John Hobs	13 Days att Same		13	0
Will Fancourt	16 Days at 10[d] att Same &. Senes for do		13	4

March ye 12 1749/50 [1750]

John Fancourt	92 Days making of frames for ye Senes and other work a bout them	6	18	0
Will Fancourt	52 Days att Same at 1s Per day	2	12	0
John Hobs	25 Days att Same Senes for do	1	5	0
John Fancourt	35 Days framing y.e Roofe of the New Bewlding	2	12	6
Will Fancourt	69 Days att Same	3	9	0
John Hobs	89 Days att Same Roofing for do	4	9	0
John Fancourt	54 Days att ye Enside work	4	1	0
Will Fancourt	30 Days att ye Same	1	10	0
John Hobs	40 Days att ye Same Enside work	2	0	0
John Fancourt	3 Days Setting up ye Stage in Chapel and t[a]king of it down		4	6
Will Fancourt	2 Days att Same		2	0
John Hobs	2 Days att Same & Stage for do		2	0
John Fancourt	25 Days making of a new Pare of Gates	1	17	6
John Fancourt	30 Days making of a new Stage and Setting up	2	5	0
Will Fancourt	30 Days att Same	1	10	0
John Hobs	30 Days att Same Stage for d.o	1	10	0

[c] [Another bill from John Fancort]
Began Decem 1750 and Ended march 1751

		£	s.	d.
John Fancourt	44 Days Setting up Scens in ye hall and Repairing of them	3	6	0
Jon Hobs	39 Days at Same	1	19	0
Will fancourt	26 Days at Sam and Scens	1	6	0
		£6	11s.	0d.

Turn Over The / Receipt is on ye other / Side

Dit^o A Bill work In ye Gardens	7	7	6
Dit^o A Bill work In ye House	13	5	2
Sum Total	84	14	11

[Received on 11 August 1751 by 'John Fan Courett']

Commentary

Three bills from John Fancort, a carpenter who evidently headed a flexible group of workmen, some of whom occasionally submitted bills independently. The spelling of his surname varies widely in the documents but is standardised in these commentaries.

The first bill [a] is dated November 1748 and headed 'N.º 2'; nothing is known of 'N.º 1'. // The first section, concerning the erection, decoration and dismantling of scenery in the garden in July 1748, undoubtedly refers to that summer's performances of *Comus* (see above, pp. 41–2). // The second and third sections (undated) relate to the erection of scenery in the Hall on two other occasions, possibly later in 1748 or in 1749. // Most of Fancort's men earned a shilling a day. Will Fancort, possibly John's son, received only sixpence a day and must have been an apprentice (see above, 8); his rate increased over the next two years (see below).

Bill [b], covering the fifteen months from September 1749 to December 1750, refers to further work on scenery and stages and to other carpentry jobs on the estate. // The latter include the construction of a bookcase, work on a new building (roof and interior) and the making of gates. // The stage that was put up (and taken down) in the chapel could conceivably have been for the concert that was given there on Sunday 2 September 1750 (see 21). // The new stage mentioned near the end may have been the one painted by Samuel Goodwin (2). // By September 1749 John Fancort was earning 1s. 6d per day. Will Fancort's rate had gone up to tenpence a day by December 1750 and to a shilling by March 1751.

The third bill [c] indicates that plays were being staged at the Hall during the last few months of Gainsborough's life.

The last three lines of the transcription cannot be fully explained. The first line (£7 7s. 6d.) refers to the total of bill 15[a]. The source of the other two amounts is not known: perhaps they derive from Fancort's (lost) bill 'N.º 1'.

An Elizabeth Fancort and an Ann Fancourt are recorded as working at Exton in 1760 and 1765, respectively ('List of Servants 1751–1772': ROLLR, DE3214/8528).

16. DE3214/10188/109

A Bill For y.ᵉ Right Honᵇˡᵉ Earl of Gainsborough

Began march yᵉ 18 1750 and Ended December yᵉ [blank] 1750. Phill. Gann

	£	s.	d.
Order of M.ʳ Jackson			
40 Days and a Half making of framess for y.ᵉ Scenes and other work a Bout them at 12:ᵈ	2	0	6
50 Days framing y.ᵉ Roof of yᵉ New Building ... &c	2	10	0
60 Days at yᵉ Enside work	3	0	0
30 Days making of a New Stage &c	1	10	0
17 Days making yᵉ new Gates & other Jobs		17	0
	£9	17s.	6d.
Examin'd & Allow'd per Wᵐ Jackson a former Bill Dito	2	1	0
	£11	18s.	6d.

[Paid by H. Cumbrey and receipted by Phillip Gann on 11 August 1751]

Commentary

A bill from Phillip Gann, a carpenter who had been a member of John Fancort's team in July 1748 (see 15[a]1). // The references in the present bill to frames for scenery, the roof and the interior of a new building, a new stage and new gates indicate that he also worked alongside John and Will Fancort and John Hobs in the period from March to December 1750 (15[b]). // The new stage may have been the one mentioned by John Fancort in 15[b] and painted by Samuel Goodwin (2). // William Jackson, who commissioned Gann's work and approved his bill, had also authorised Kell Berrey's work in 1748–9 (see 1).

17. DE3214/10188/110

[a] A Bill for the R.[tt] Hon.[ble] Earl of Gainsborough from John Newbould for the plays

1749		£	s.	d.
dec:[r] 6	making my lord a blue Coate for sr. Toby		5	0
	thrid 3.[d] buckram 8.[d] Canvis 3.[d]		1	1
	making a belley [an apron] 12.[d] thrid 2.[d]		1	2
	altering L.[d] Cams: danceing dress 18.[d] thrid & silk 3.[d]		1	9
9	making the Clowns dress 3[s]: 6.[d] thrid 3.[d]		3	9
12	half a day geting dresses ready			6
	thrid & silk			2
13	leting out a brown Camblit Coate & taking it in again			6
19	half a day			6
26	making a new Curtain 3[s]. 1 oz: & half of thrid 4[d] ½		3	4½
29	altering the old Curtain & for thrid		1	0
	John Low half a day fitting side sceeings 6.[d] thrid 1.[d]			7
30	half a day fiting the new Chamber sceeing 6.[d] thrid 1.[d]			7
	making a Corporals Coate		3	6
	thrid 4.[d] 24 y:[ds] binding of 1.[d]		2	4
	2 dozen & half of Coate buttons at 8.[d]		1	8

1750				
Jan 1	making 4 black Cloaks 2.[s] thrid 6.[d]		2	6
2	half a day altering seeings			6
	making 3 sword belts		1	6
	taking off a pair of waistcoate sleeves & leting down a pair of Coate Sleeves M:[r] proby			3
3	leting out a black Coate for M:[r] hurst			3
	taking in a black Coate for M:[r] snow			2
	my self and man Each half a day geting dresses ready		1	0
4	my self all day mending sr John Fallstafs dress & geting other dresses ready		1	0
6	new buttoning S:[r] tobys Coate 2.[d] thrid 1.[d]			3
	my self half a day			6
9	half a day			6
10	mending 3 sword scabbards			4
	whale bone			3
	half a day			6
12	half a day			6
13	half a day			6
	thrid & silk			4
16	my self & man Each half a day geting dresses ready & laying others by		1	0
	leting out a black Coate of m:[r] Cumbreys as m:[r] snow had			3

Appendix II 93

[Omitted: claims for days and half-days of unspecified work]

Date	Description	£	s.	d.
[March 27]	taking the buttons off of s.ʳ tobys Coate & seting them upon a scarlet freize waistcoate 2.ᵈ thrid 1.ᵈ			3
april 16	began to Cover the sceeings my self 4 days		4	0
	4 oz: brown thrid			8
	my man 4 days & half		4	6
	prentis 4 days & half at 8.ᵈ		3	0
April 25	half a day geting dresses ready			6
	leting down a brown & gold frock & leting down the sleeves for m.ʳ proby			3
28	half a day seaming Cloth to part the barn			6
	thrid 1 oz			2
30	seting sleeves upon a scarlet imbroidered waistcoate			2
June 25	seaming Cloth to Cover 2 large frames & nailing the Cloth upon the frames my self 1 day		1	0
	thrid			2
Augˢᵗ 21	Covering 2 frames half a day 6.ᵈ thrid 1.ᵈ			7
	Nº 3	£3	0s.	3½d.
			R.ᵗ	

[b] A Bill for the R:ᵗᵗ Hon:ᵇˡᵉ Earl of Gainsborough from John Newbould for work for the Plays

1750		£	s.	d.
Nov:ʳ 8	Covering 6 side sceenngs my self 2 days my man 1 day		3	0
	thrid			6
17	Covering the sound board my self 1 day		1	0
	prentis 1 day 9.ᵈ thrid 2.ᵈ			11
	altering L.ᵈ Cam: a blue Coate puting hair shapes & madding		2	0
	hair shapes & coverings		1	6
	cleaning the face & buttons		1	0
19	making 2 back sceeings 12.ᵈ thrid 2.ᵈ		1	2
22	Covering 3 frames for the front of yᵉ stage			6
26	altering a sailors dress for w:ᵐ willson			4
	altering a gaurds [sic] dress do: 6.ᵈ thrid 1ᵈ.½			7½
	altering a Coate & waistcoate for Robert Pragnell		1	0
	thrid			2
	mending a black Coate of my lords			2
29	making Curtains for the hall doors a Curtain for the stair Case Covering a frame do: & 2 frames for windows for the stage new buttoning a Coate for sr: toby altering a Coate & waistcoate for w:m moulten & altering sceeings my self 3 days		3	0
	my man 3 days		3	0
	Prentis 2 days		1	6
dec:ʳ 4	stiffning the brest of a black Coate 3⁽ᵈ⁾ buckram 4.ᵈ thrid 1.ᵈ			8
5	half a day laying dresses by			6
7	my self all day geting dresses ready		1	0

94 *Appendix II*

8	half a day laying dresses by		6
17	making the hall window Curtains & putting them up & Covering a frame & door for the stair case		
	my self 3 days ½	3	6
	my man 3 days	3	0
	Oliver Clingworth 3 days	3	0
	my prentis 3 days	2	3
	tho: Sherman 2 days	1	0
	half oz: green silk	1	2
Dec:[r] 22	taking the stage Curtain down making it broader & puting it up again 1 day	1	0
26	Cleaning a star some silver Ribbon & a hat lace	1	0
27	half a day geting dresses ready		6

[Omitted: claims for days and half-days of unspecified work]

1751

Jan 7	taking a Coate shorter for John Brown Esq:[e]		6
14	my man half a day altering sceeings		6
	thrid		1
Jan 15	altering mr. Blathwaits dress 6.[d] thrid 1.[d]		7
16	altering L.[d] Cams: dress for the page		6
	altering S:[r] John fallstafs boots		6
	altering the breeches		3
	making 3 great Coats	6	0
	buckram & Canvis 8.[d] Each	2	0
	making lady Juleys dress 2.[s] 6.[d] thrid 3.[d] silk 2.[d]	2	11
18	my self all day	1	0
	mending S:[r] John fallstafs sword scabbard		4
	whale bone		2

[Claims for days and half-days of unspecified work]

29	half a day laying the dresses by		6
		£3 2s. 6½d.	

[Wrapper, inside:]
   An Abstract of Jo.[n] Newboulds Bills for Work Done
for the R.[t] Hon.[ble] The Earl of Gainsborough To Lady Day 1751
The Bills Comes Too £38 8s. 7d.
August y.[e] 11: 1751 Rec.[d] of H. Cumbrey [autograph signature:]
John Newbould

[Outside:]
   Jo.[n] Newboulds abstract of bills £38 8s. 7d.
   Paid all demands to Lady Day [25 March]. 1751.

Appendix II   95

Commentary

Two bills from John Newbould for work 'for the plays', the first [a] covering the period from 6 December 1749 to 21 August 1750, the second [b] from 8 November 1750 to 29 January 1751. // Newbould's work consisted predominantly of making and altering costumes and curtains, 'getting dresses ready', 'laying dresses by' and covering frames for scenery. // Both bills mention Sir Toby (presumably Sir Toby Belch in Shakespeare's *Twelfth Night*) and Sir John Falstaff. Taken together with the 'Inn Yard' (2), the references to Falstaff must relate to *Henry IV, Part I*, which therefore appears to have been performed at Exton. // The bills also name individuals for whom costumes were made, including Gainsborough's son Baptist (Viscount Campden) and his daughter Juliana ('Lady Juley', 16 January 1751); a play had been bound for Juliana on 11 December 1750 (see 4). The other named individuals were probably friends of the family or members of the household: Mr Blathwayt (15 January 1751) also appears in documents 9 and 11, Mr Cumbrey (16 January 1750) in 16.

---

18. DE3214/10329

[A handwritten book of poems, compiled *c*. 1745–52 (most of the poems are dated at the end). Upright, *c*. 20.7 x 13 cm, pp. 34, of which pp. 2–25 are numbered; marbled paper covers (perished).]

[Hand 1 (small, faint):]

[p. 1]	On my favourite Seat In the Walnut Tree Walk In Exton Gardens / 1745
3	On seeing a fading Lime Tree / Address'd to Ophelia / 1746
5	Wrote upon a Seat under a Grove of Yew-Trees in Exton Gardens / 1747
5	Jenny's Thimble An Extempore Simile / 1747
6	An Extempore Thought on the Vicissitudes of Life / 1748
8	Ode on Fortune / 1749
9	The Fall of the Mulberry / Address'd to Castalio / 1749
11	A Panegyrick on y[e] History of Clarissa / Alterd from Pope's Prologue to Cato / 1749
14	To some young Ladies singing a Ballad on May Day / 1750
15	A Riddle, and The Answer / 1749
17	A Riddle
20	To Ophelia / ON FLORIO'S Birth-Day / 1750
22	On seeing a Lady's Name wrote on a Leaf. Address'd to her by Florio / 1751
23	The Petition of Time to Julio / Occasion'd by a Gentleman leaving his Watch behind him, w.[ch] a Lady found, and sent him back wth these verses.
25	The Answer to Leonora

[Hand 2 (larger, darker):]

[26–27 quatrains in iambic pentameters]
[28–31] A Paraphrase on the 3[d] Ode of the / Second Book of Horace /
          To J____ N____ Esq
[31–4 empty]

Commentary

The poems on pp. 1–25 appear to have been entered, possibly by the poet, in the order in which they were written. The latest date given, 1751, is the year in which Lord Gainsborough died: either he was (one of) the poet(s) or his death robbed the poet(s) of the desire to carry on writing. // The dedicatee of the paraphrase on pp. 28–31 may have been Gainsborough's brother, James Noel; if he was, this paraphrase – and perhaps the whole manuscript – must have been completed before his death on 17 June 1752. // The poems on pp. 1 and 5 extol the Exton gardens; 'Jenny' (p. 5) was Gainsborough's daughter Jane (born 1733), whom Benjamin Martyn called 'Lady Jenny' in 1748 (Matthews, 'Unpublished Letters', 268; *Handel: Collected Documents*, iv, 588–90).

Other poems refer to literary works: Ophelia (pp. 3 and 20) is a character in *Hamlet*, which was purchased by Gainsborough on 23 March 1750 (4); 'Castalio' (p. 9) is a character in Thomas Otway's *The Orphan*, acquired on 13 March 1750 (4); Samuel Richardson's novel *Clarissa* (p. 11), published in seven volumes in 1747–8, was purchased on 23 November 1750 (5); the 'Panegyrick' (p. 11) is based on Pope's 'Prologue to Mr. Addison's Tragedy of *Cato*', a play that dates from 1713.

Julio and Leonora (pp. 23 and 25) are characters in Theobald's play *Double Falsehood*, which was bought on 2 January 1749 (5) and evidently staged at Exton (see above, document 2 and pp. 46–9). These parts may have been played by members of Gainsborough's family or household; that of Julio, a name that recurs in document 19, may have been taken by his brother James. // Florio (p. 20) is the name by which, in *Double Falsehood* (Act V, scene 2), the female character Violante identifies herself when disguised as a boy.

---

19. DE3214/10330

The Bowling-Green

[A poem about the bowling green at Exton – the game itself, those who played it there and, by extension, the fickleness of fortune. Reference is made to twenty-nine players. Fourteen names are given in full; five are suggested by first and last letters, linked by 'plus' signs, and the remainder by first, last and sometimes intervening letters joined by horizontal lines:]

Julio	Wilson	B_____le**
Mountford	N++n	C_____y
Garcia	D++y	Spicer
Darus	B++rs	E____l
Backwell	S___th___	Cumbrey
C_____ll	B++n	Dipper
Browning*	R++r	G____l
Beasely*	W_____n	W____d
Ward*	T_____d	N__r__m__n
Hughes	Great Earl	

* 3 Labourers y:ᵗ work in y.ᵉ Garden. ** a peacefull man of God.

Commentary

Julio, the first name in the list, is a character in Theobald's play *Double Falsehood* (see 18). // 'Cumbrey' is presumably the Mr H. Cumbrey who took part in amateur theatricals at Exton (17[a] and 17[b]) and paid the carpenter Phillip Gann (16). // 'B++n' could conceivably be the Mr Brown who played a part in the staging of *Double Falsehood* (see above, p. 46) and/or the John Brown for whom a coat was shortened by John Newbould in January 1751 (17[b]). The bowling green at Exton was in use by the summer of 1750 (see below, 21). It may have been created by Lord Gainsborough, who is probably the 'Great Earl' mentioned at the foot of the middle column above.

20. DE3214/10350

Esther

Commentary

A manuscript libretto of Handel's oratorio, presumably prepared for a performance at Exton (of which no other evidence is known) and briefly described in *Handel: Collected Documents*, iv, 594. // The characters are: Assueras (sic), Esther, Habdonah, Haman, Mordecai, 1st Israelite, 2nd Israelite and Officer; there is no Israelite Boy or Priest of the Israelites.

The libretto is closer to the 1720 (Cannons) version of the work than to the 1732 version, but borrows features from both. It is divided into three acts, as in 1732, but lacks that version's Act I scenes 1, 2 and 4, Act II scene 1, the duet 'Blessings descend on downy wings' (II/2), the air 'Heaven has lent her every charm' (II/4) and four numbers in III/4.

The libretto begins with the recitative "Tis greater far to spare' (I/3 in 1732) and omits two numbers in the Cannons scene 2 (the chorus 'Shall we of servitude complain' and the air 'Praise the Lord with cheerful noise'). It also excludes the air 'Sing songs of praise' which, although it appears in Howard Serwer's edition of the 1718 version of *Esther* (Hallische Händel-Ausgabe, ser. I, vol. 8), was probably not part of the finished Cannons version of *c*. 1720, being replaced by 'Praise the Lord' (see John H. Roberts, 'The Composition of Handel's *Esther*, 1718–1720', *Händel-Jahrbuch*, 55 (2009), 353–90, at 373–5). The Exton libretto also replaces the chorus at the end of scene 5 ('Virtue, truth and innocence') with a repeat of 'Save us, O Lord' (scene 4). The accompagnato 'Turn not, O queen' and the air 'Flatt'ring tongue' (both in scene 6) are omitted. The closing sequence, too, is altered: the air 'How art thou fall'n' is followed by 'I'll proclaim the wondrous story' (1732), but here this duet is framed by two new pieces of recitative ('Howe'er success' and 'Rejoice, Judea', respectively). Finally, the concluding chorus

98 *Appendix II*

('The Lord our enemy has slain') is replaced by the last movement of *Joshua* ('The great Jehovah is our awful theme').

The Exton libretto cannot date from before 19 August 1747, when *Joshua* was completed, or, more likely, from before 9 March 1748, when it was first performed. More realistically, the libretto may date from after April-May 1748, when Gainsborough had a score of *Joshua* bound (7). // It is not known whether *Esther* was performed at Exton, but if it was, the most likely dates are the summer of 1748, when *Comus* was revived and Margaret Smith attended 'one of their Oratorios' (see, p. 2), and that of 1749; it does not appear to have been performed in summer 1750 (see 21).

21. DE3214/10351

[A small sheet of paper, folded once and torn]

Went to Exton Tusday Aug the 28 1750

That Evening went in to the park had Musick as ye passed by in three different Trees returned and had A Consert by the whole Band

Wednesday ye 29th

had a Consert after Brakefast then went out of doors Set down at one of the fine woods walked through it to return to Dress In the Evening had Alexanders Feast performed

Thursday ye 30th walked in the Morning In the Evening had the Oratora of Sampson Performed

Friday ye 31th Morning Sampson again In the Evening the gentlemen Bowled till Dark and then a Concert of Musick of the whole Band till Super

Saturday Sep[tem]ber ye 1th Morning Sampson Again In the Evening the gentlemen Bowled till Dark and then a Concert of Musick till 9 o'Clock Super and went in to the Garden which was Illuminated and Fire Works Displayed till past 12 o Clock

Sunday ye 2th was to the Queens Funeral Anthem and othere proper Musick in the Chapel

Commentary

An anonymous account of a festival of music at Exton in the summer of 1750 that consisted of four concerts, Handel's *Alexander's Feast* and *Samson*, and a performance of his funeral anthem for Queen Caroline (*The Ways of Zion do mourn*) and of 'othere proper Musick' in the chapel. // 'The whole Band' presumably comprised strings and harpsichord, with oboes and bassoon(s). // *Samson* is unlikely to have been performed complete on three consecutive days: it was probably presented in instalments, one act per day. This performance must be related to the purchase of a dozen wordbooks of the oratorio (11), the copying of part of a chorus (11) and of a vocal part for Viscount Campden (4), and the binding of the score (7). // The funeral anthem (1737) had been re-used by Handel, with different words, as the first Part of *Israel in Egypt* (1739). // Bowls was evidently a favourite pastime at Exton (see 19).

Index to the Documents

This index comprises lists of the books, music and musical instruments, plays and theatrical items referred to in the twenty-one documents above. Prints (or 'views') are discussed in the Commentaries; paper and other miscellaneous items are excluded. Most of the entries for books and plays indicate purchases; some relate to binding. The numbers at the end of the entries denote the documents in which the items appear.

Books

The index of books is essentially a key to the identity of the works that are mentioned in the documents. It excludes editions of individual plays, which are listed separately below, but includes collected editions of plays (e.g., the *Works* of William Congreve).

The references to books in the documents are mostly incomplete or imprecise. The attempt to establish their identity was facilitated by a variety of resources, including the British Library catalogue, Eighteenth Century Collections Online, Gallica, JISC Library Hub Discover, and WorldCat.

In this index the books are divided into three lists. 'Positive identifications' are arranged in alphabetical order, mostly by author. If the author is not named in the source but has been identified, the list cites the wording from the document and gives a cross-reference to the author's name; if the author's identity is unknown, the work is listed under '[Anon.]'. Each entry in the list includes the date of the last known edition before the date of billing in the document; in some cases the date of one or more earlier editions is added. The place of publication, unless otherwise specified, was London.

The second list, 'Uncertain identifications', includes document entries for which at least one plausible but not entirely convincing match has been found; difficult cases are discussed in the Commentaries above.

The third section lists entries not yet identified.

100 *Appendix II*

Positive Identifications (short titles)

'Account of Madera': *see* Alcoforado

'Actor': *see* Hill

Addison, Joseph, *The Evidences of the Christian Religion* (1730); 4th edn (1745) 5

Æsop, *The Fables* [...] *Newly done into English* [by Samuel Croxall ...] *Illustrated with Cutts* (1722), 5th edn (1747) 7

Aglionby, William, *Painting illustrated in Three Diallogues* [...] *with the Lives of the Most Eminent Painters* (1685), or *Choice Observations on the art of Painting* [...] *with Vasari's Lives of the Most Eminent Painters* (1719) 10

Albinus, Bernhard Siegfried, *Tabulæ sceleti et musculorum corporis humani* (1747–9) 7

Alcoforado, Francisco, *An Historical Relation of the First Discovery of the Isle of Madera* (1675), as *An Historical Account of the Discovery of the Island of Madeira* (1750) 5

Aler, Paul, *Gradus ad Parnassum, sive Novus synonymorum, epithetorum, phrasium poeticarum ac versuum Thesaurus* [...] *in usum studiosæ juventutis* (1680); [11th?] edn (1749) 5

'Amours of Zeokinizul': *see* Jolyot de Crébillon

'An Attempt': *see* [Holt]

'Angola histoire indienne': *see* La Morlière

[Annet, Peter], *The History and Character of St Paul, Examined* (1748) 7

[Anon.], *The Advantages of the Difinitive [sic] Treaty, to the People of Great-Britain, demonstrated*, 2nd edn (1749) 5

———, *The Antient and Present State of Military Law in Great Britain consider'd* (1749) 5

———, *An Apology for a Late Resignation* [of Philip Dormer Stanhope, 4th Earl of Chesterfield, as Secretary of State for the Northern Department] (1748) 7

———, *Arithmetick made so Easy, that it may be Learned without a Master* [...] *for the Use of Schools* [...] *Translated from the French by Thomas Fletcher* (1727), 2nd edn (1740) 5

———, *The Case of M. [Bertrand-François Mahé] de la Bourdonnais. In a Letter to a Friend* (1748) 7

———, *The Court and City Register for the Year 1750*, 11th edn [1750] 5

———, *The Gallant Companion, or, An Antidote for the Hyp and Vapours* (1746) 7

———, *An Historical, Genealogical and Classical Dictionary*, 2 vols. (1743) 7

———, *The Life and Adventures of Bampfylde-Moore Carew, the Noted Devonshire Stroller and Dog-stealer* (1745); later edn as *An Apology for the Life of Bampfylde-Moore Carew* [...] *Commonly Known* [...] *by the title of King of the Beggars* [1749] 5

———, *The Life of Augustus Cæsar* [...] *Translated from the French*, 2 vols. (1748) 5

———, *Musæ anglicanæ, sive Poemata quædam melioris notæ, seu hactenus inedita, seu sparsim edita*, 4th and 5th edns, ed. Vincent Bourne, 2 vols. (1741) 5

———, *The Polite Arts, or, A Dissertation on Poetry, Painting, Musick, Architecture, and Eloquence* (1749) 5

———, *Reasons for giving up Gibraltar* [...] *and a Summary of Its State, Situation, and Government* (1749) 5

———, *The Report of the Proceedings and Opinion of the Board of General Officers, on their Examination into the Conduct* [...] *of Lieutenant-General Sir John Cope* [...] *Colonel Peregrine Lascelles, and Brigadier-General Thomas Fowke, from the*

[...] *Rebellion in North-Britain in the Year 1745 till the Action at Preston-Pans Inclusive*, 3rd edn (1749) 7

——, *Thoughts on the Present Laws for Preserving the Game* [...] *and Some Methods* [...] *for Making a Game Law* (1750) 7

——, *The Traveller's Pocket-Companion: or, A Compleat Description of the Roads* [...] *from London* [...] *a New Survey-Map, which shews the Market-Days* [...] *an Account of the Expences of sending a Letter or Pacquet by Express from the General Post-Office* (1741), another edn (1743) 5

——, *The True and Real Interest of Great Britain Impartially Considered, with regard to the impending Rupture among the Northern Powers* (1749) 5

——, *A True Dialogue between Thomas Jones, a Trooper, lately returned from Germany, and John Smith, a Serjeant in the First Regiment of Foot-Guards* (1743); another edn as *A True Dialogue between Thomas Jones, a Life-Guard-man, and John Smith, late a Serjeant in the First Regiment of Foot-Guards* (1749) 10

——, *Two Letters from a Physician in London, to a Gentleman in Bath* (1749) 5

——, *The Universal Pocket-Book* [...] *containing* [...] *A Map of the World* [...] *An Historical Table* [...] *A Map of England* [...] *A List of the House of Peers* [...] *The Gardiner's Monthly Director* [...] *A New Perpetual Almanack* [...] *A New Plan of London* [...] *A List of Places at Court. A Table of Simple Interest* [...] *Rates of Watermen, Coachmen and Chairmen,* [*Details*] *of the General* [...] *and Penny-Post* [...] *The Prices of* [...] *Bricklayers, Masons, Joiners* [*etc.* ...] *An Account of all the Stagecoaches and Carriers in England and Scotland* (1740), 5th edn (1745) 5

——, *A Voyage to the South-Seas, and to many other Parts of the World, performed from the month of September in the Year 1740 to June 1744, by Commodore* [*George*] *Anson* [...] *by an Officer of the Squadron* (1744) 5, 7

Anson, George: *see* [Anon.], *A Voyage*

'Antiq[uities] of Windsor': *see* Pote

Anville, Jean Baptiste Bourguignon d', *Twelve Maps of Ancient Geography* [...] *designed for the Explanation of Mr.* [*Charles*] *Rollin's Ancient History* (1750) 5

Arbuthnot, John, *An Essay Concerning the Effects of Air on Human Bodies* (1733) 10
——: *see* Miscellanies

Atterbury, Francis, *Sermons and Discourses on several Subjects and Occasions*; 5th edn, 2 vols. (1740) 5

Bailey, Nathan, *Dictionarium Britannicum, or a More Compleat Universal Etymological English Dictionary than any extant* (1730), 2nd edn (1736) 5

Banier, Antoine (abbé), *The Mythology and Fables of the Ancients* [...] *Translated from the original French*, 4 vols. (1739–40) 5

[Blackwell, Thomas], *Letters concerning Mythology* (1748) 10

Bolingbroke (Viscount): *see* St John, Henry

Bourdonnais: *see* Mahé de la Bourdonnais

Bowen, Emanuel, *A Complete System of Geography* [...] *Illustrated with Seventy Maps* (1744), [2nd edn], 2 vols. (1747) 5

Caesar, Julius, *C. Julii Caesaris quae extant: Accuratissimè cum libris editis & MSS. optimis collata, recognita & correcta. Accesserunt annotationes Samuelis Clarke* [3 issues] (1712, 1720, 1739) 5

'Cannons of Criticisme': *see* Edwards, Thomas

'Castle of Indolence': *see* Thomson

'Character of King Charles II, The': *see* Savile

Chesterfield, 4th Earl of: *see* [Anon.], *An Apology*
'Child's Delight': *see* Keach
Cibber, Colley, *An Apology for the Life* [...] *With an Historical View of the Stage during his own Time* (1740), 3rd edn (1750) 5
Cicero, Marcus Tullius, *Orations* (1741) and *Morals* (1744), trans. William Guthrie 5
'Clarissa': *see* Richardson
'Classical Dictionary': *see* [Anon.], *An Historical*
Cleland, John, *Memoirs of a Woman of Pleasure* [Fanny Hill], 2 vols. (1748, 1749) 5
'Compleat angler': *see* Walton
'Compleat fisher': *see* [Smith]
Congreve, William, *The Works* (1710), 5th edn (1730) 7
'Conquest of Mexico': *see* Ribadeneyra
Cousteil, Isaac, *A French Idiomatical and Critical Vocabulary* (1748) 5
'Croxalls Fables': see æsop
De Curli, *The Life and Amours of Owen Tideric, Prince of Wales, otherwise Owen Tudor* [...] *First wrote in French* [...] *and Now translated into English* (1751) 7
Defoe, Daniel, *Robinson Crusoe* (1719), 9th edn, 2 vols. (1747) 7
'Description of Heraclea': *see* Venuti
'Dialogue T. Jones and J. Smith': *see* [Anon.], *A True Dialogue*
'Dialogues': *see* Gilpin
Dryden, John, *The Dramatick Works*, ed. William Congreve, 6 vols. (1735) 7
Du Pin, Louis Ellies, *An Exact History of the Life, Death & Acts of our Blessed Saviour Jesus Christ* (1694); 3rd edn as *The Evangelical History, or The Life of our Blessed Saviour Jesus Christ* [...] *Written in French* [...] *and Englished* (1703; repr. to 1732)
Dubos, Jean-Baptiste (abbé), *Critical Reflections on Poetry, Painting and Music*, trans. Thomas Nugent, 3 vols. (1748) 10
Edwards, George, *A Natural History of Birds* [...] *Engrav'd on Fifty-Two Copper Plates* [...] *and Exactly Colour'd*, 4 parts in 2 vols. (1743–50) 10
———, *A Natural History of Birds, the Most of Which have not hitherto been Figured or Described*, Parts III and IV (1750–51, 1751) 5
Edwards, Thomas, *A Supplement to Mr. Warburton's Edition of Shakespear. Being the Canons of Criticism, and Glossary* (1748) 5
'Essay on Air on Bodies': *see* Arbuthnot
'Essay on Design': *see* Gwynn
'Essay on Dilacacy': *see* Lancaster
Fielding, Henry, *The History of Tom Jones, a Foundling*, 6 vols. (1749) 5, 10
Fielding, Sarah, *The Governess, or Little Female Academy* (1749) 5
'Fitzosborne': *see* Melmoth
'Fletcher': *see* [Anon.], *Arithmetick*
Florus, Annæus Lucius, *Rerum romanorum epitome: or, An Abridgment of the Roman History* [...] *for the Use of Schools*, ed. John Stirling (1738) 5
'Free & important disquisition': *see* [Jones]
'French Vocabilary': *see* Cousteil
'Frye Interest': *see* [Anon.], *The True and Real Interest*
Gay, John: *see* Miscellanies
'Gill Blass': *see* Lesage
Gilpin, William, *A Dialogue upon the Gardens of the Right Honourable the Lord Viscount Cobham, at Stow in Buckinghamshire* (1748), 2nd edn (1749) 5

Godwin, Francis, *De præsulibus Angliæ commentarius: omnium episcoporum necnon et cardinalium ejusdem gentis, nomina, tempora, seriem atque actiones maxime memorabiles* (1616), ed. and continued by William Richardson (Cambridge, 1743) 5
'Governess': *see* Fielding, Sarah
'Græ. Grammat': see [Pote]
[Grafigny, Françoise Paule Huguet de], *Letters written by a Peruvian Princess. Translated from the French* (1748); rev. and corr. edn, *To which is now first added, the Sequel of the Peruvian Letters* (1749) 5
Guthrie, William, *A General History of England, from the Invasion of the Romans under Julius Cæsar to the late Revolution in MDCLXXXVIII*, 3 vols. (1744, 1747, 1751) 5
Gwynn, John, *An Essay on Design, including Proposals for Erecting a Public Academy [...] for Educating the British Youth in Drawing and the several Arts depending there on* (1749) 10
Hartley, David, *Observations on Man, his Frame, his Duty and his Expectations*, 2 vols. (1749) 5, 10
Haywood, Eliza Fowler, *The Fruitless Enquiry: being a collection of Histories and Occurrences [...] of a Lady in her Search after Happiness* (1727) 5
Herodian, *History of his own Times, or of the Roman Empire after Marcus*, trans. J. Hart (1749) 5
Hill, John, *The Actor: A Treatise on the Art of Playing* (1750) 5
'History of [...] St Paul': *see* [Annet]
Holinshed, Raphael, and others, *The First and Second Volumes of Chronicles [...] Now [...] continued [...] to [...] 1586 by John Hooker [...] and others* (1728) 5
———, *The Third Volume of Chronicles, Beginning at Duke William the Norman [...] Now [...] continued [...] to [...] 1586* (1728) 5
[Holt, John], *Remarks on The Tempest, or An Attempt to Rescue Shakespear* [1750] 5
Homer, *The Odyssey*, trans. Alexander Pope, 5 vols. (1725–6) 5, 10
Hooker, John: *see* Holinshed
Horace [Quinti Horatii Flacci], *Opera*, 2 vols. (1749) 5
Hughes, John, *Poems on Several Occasions, with some Select Essays in Prose*, 2 vols. (1735) 5
Jolyot de Crébillon, Claude Prosper, *The Sopha: a Moral Tale. Translated from the French* (1742) 7
———, *The Amours of Zeokinizul, King of the Kofrans. Translated from the Arabic of [...] Krinelbol* (1749) 5
Jones, John, *Free and candid Disquisitions relating to the Church of England, and the Means of Advancing Religion therein* (1749), 2nd edn (1750) 5
Keach, Benjamin, *The Child's Delight: containing a Scripture Catechism* (1683); 25th edn as *Instructions for Children: or, The Child's and Youth's Delight [...] with a Scripture Catechism* (1738) 5
La Condamine, Charles-Marie de, *A Succinct Abridgment of a Voyage made within the Inland Parts of South-America: from the Coasts of the South-sea to the Coasts of Brazil and Guiana, down the River of Amazons* (1747) 5
La Morlière, Charles-Jacques-Louis-Auguste Rochette de, *Angola, histoire indienne: ouvrage sans vrai-semblance* (three possible edns: Paris, 1746, 1748 and 1749) 5

La Rochefoucauld, François (duc de), *Moral Maxims and Reflections* [...] *Written in French* [...] *Now made English*, 2nd edn (1706) 5
Lancaster, Nathaniel, *The Plan of an Essay upon Delicacy* (1748) 5
Lens, Bernard, *For the curious Young Gentlemen and Ladies that study* [...] *the Noble* [...] *Art of Drawing* [...] *A New and Compleat Drawing Book* [...] *in Sixty Two Copper-Plates* (1750) 5
Lesage [Le Sage], Alain-René, *Histoire de Gil Blas de Santillane* (Paris, 1715–35), trans. Tobias Smollett as *The History of Gil Blas*, 5th edn, 4 vols. (1744–6) 5
'L'Esprit du loix': *see* Montesquieu
'L[ette]r ab[ou]t Exam[ination]: *see* [Anon.], *The Report*
'Letters concerning Mythology': *see* [Blackwell]
'Lexicon Etymolog[ical]': *see* Bailey
Littleton, Adam, *Latin Dictionary, in Four Parts*, 6th edn (1735) 5
Littleton, Edward, *Sermons upon Several Practical Subjects. By the late Reverend Edward Littleton, L.L.D. Fellow of Eton-College* [...] *Published by subscription, for the benefit of his Widow and Children*, vol. 1 (1735); 3rd edn (1749) 10
Lobb, Theophilus, *Letters relating to the Plague and other Contagious Distempers* (1745) 5
[Lockman, John], *A New Roman History by Question and Answer* [...] *Designed principally for Schools*, 3rd edn (1749) 5
'Lord Bolingbroke's Letters': *see* St John, Henry
Lucan (Lucanus, Marcus Annaeus), *Pharsalia: sive de bello civili inter Cæsarem et Pompeium libri decem*, ed. Michael Maittaire (1719) 5
'Maps of Geog[raphy]': *see* Bowen
Melmoth, William, the younger, *Letters on Several Subjects. By the late Sir Thomas Fitzosborne* [pseud.]. *To which is added* [...] *A Dialogue upon Oratory attributed to Quinctilian*, 2 vols. (1748, 1749) 5, 7, 10
'Memoirs 2 vols': *see* Pilkington, Laetitia
'Memoirs of a Woman of Pleasure': *see* Cleland
Miller, Philip, *The Gardeners and Florists Dictionary* (1724), 3rd edn, corrected, as *The Gardeners Dictionary*, 2 vols., fol. (1737, 1739) 5
Miscellanies by Dr Swift, Dr Arbuthnot, Mr Pope and Mr Gay, 4 vols.; 6th edn [...], with [...] *Additional Pieces in Verse and Prose* [by Swift: vols. 5–13] (1751) 5
Molière (Jean-Baptiste Poquelin), *The Works* [...] *French and English*, 10 vols. (1739) 5
Montesquieu, Charles-Louis de Secondat (Baron de), *De l'Esprit des lois*, 2 vols. (Geneva, 1748) 5
——, *The Spirit of Laws*, trans. Thomas Nugent, 2 vols. (1748) 5
[Moss, Charles], *The Sequel of the Tryal of the Witnesses of the Resurrection. Being an Answer to* [... P. Annet]. *Revised by the Author of The Tryal of the Witnesses* [T. Sherlock] (1749) 5
Muller, John, *The Attack and Defence of Fortify'd Places* [...] *For the Use of the Royal Academy of Artillery at Woolwich* (1747) 5
'Nature displayed': *see* Pluche
Nepos, Cornelius, *The Lives of Illustrious Men. Written in Latin* [...] *and Done into English* (1684); 4th edn (1723) 5
Oudart Feudrix de Bréquigny, Louis Georges, *The History of the Revolutions in Genoa, from its Establishment to* [...] *1748*, 3 vols. (1751) 5

Ovid (Publius Ovidius Naso), *Art of Love Paraphrased, and Adapted to the Present Time* [...] Book I (1747) 7
'Owen Tudor': *see* De Curli
'Paruvian L^{rs} &c.': *see* [Grafigny]
Pascal, Blaise, *Les provinciales, ou Les Lettres écrites par Louis de Montalte* [pseud.] *à un provincial de ses amis* (Cologne, 1657); many edns (1733–8) 5
Perceval, John (Earl of Egmont), *An Examination of the Principles, and an Enquiry into the Conduct of the Two B[rothe]rs* (1749) 5
Pilkington, Laetitia, *Memoirs* [...] *wherein* [...] *All her Poems* [...] *with Anecdotes of several Eminent Persons Living and Dead*, 2 vols. (1748, 1749) 5
Pilkington, Matthew, *The Evangelical History and Harmony* (1747) 5
Pindar, *Odes* [...] *with several other pieces* [...], trans. Gilbert West (1749) 5
Pluche, Antoine-Noël, *Spectacle de la nature: or, Nature Display'd. Being Discourses on Such Particulars of Natural History as were thought proper to Excite the Curiosity, and form the Minds of Youth. Illustrated with Copperplates.* Trans. [Samuel Humphreys], (1733), 6th edn (1743–4), 7th edn (1749–50) 10
Pomey, François, *An Abridgment of Pomey's Pantheon, by way of Latin Exercise* [...] *for the Use of Schools*, ed. John Stirling (1740) 5
———, *The Pantheon, representing the fabulous Histories of the Heathen Gods and Most Illustrious Heroes*, 2nd edn, rev. Andrew Tooke (1698), 16th edn (1747) 5
Pope, Alexander, *The New Dunciad, as it was found in the Year 1741* (1742) 5
———, *see* Miscellanies
'Pope's Odyssey': *see* Homer
[Pote, Joseph], *Græcæ grammaticæ rudimenta. In usum juventutis* (Eton, 1747) 5
Pote, Joseph, *The History and Antiquities of Windsor Castle, and the Royal College, and Chapel of St. George* [...] *Illustrated with Cuts* (Eton, 1749) 5
Pozzo, Andrea, *Rules and Examples of Perspective proper for Painters and Architects* (1707; repr. [between 1730 and 1739]) 10
'Revolu[tion] of Genoa': *see* Oudart Feudrix
Ribadeneyra, Antonio de Solis y, *The History of the Conquest of Mexico by the Spaniards*, trans. Thomas Townsend, rev. Nathaniel Hooke, 2 vols. (1738) 5
Richardson, Samuel, *Clarissa, or The History of a Young Lady* (1747–8), 2nd edn (1749) 5
'Robinson Corisoe': *see* Defoe
'Rodericks Random': *see* Smollett
'Rollins History': *see* Anville
'Roman Hist[ory]': *see* [Lockman]
'Rouchf^s Maxims': *see* La Rochefoucauld
Rowning, John, *A Compendious System of Natural Philosophy* (1734), 4th edn (1744–5) 5
St John, Henry (Viscount Bolingbroke), *Letters on the Spirit of Patriotism* (1749) 10
[Sale, George, and others], *An Universal History from the Earliest Account of Time*, 21 vols. (1747–8) 5
[———], *An Universal History*, vol. 1 only 5
Salmon, Thomas, *A New Geographical and Historical Grammar* (1749) 5
———, *Modern History, or The Present State of All Nations* [...] *Illustrated with Cuts and Maps* [...] *by Hermann Moll* (1725), 3rd edn, 3 vols. (1744–6) 5
'Samaritan': *see* Yardley

'Sanby' [*recte* Sandby, William: publisher]: *see* Horace
Savile, George (Marquis of Halifax), *A Character of King Charles the Second* (1750) 5
Seed, Jeremiah, *Discourses on Several Important Subjects: To which are added Eight Sermons* (1743), 3rd edn (1747) 10
'Sequel to the Tryal': *see* [Moss]
Shakespeare, William, *The Works* [...] *Collated with the Oldest Copies, and Corrected, with Notes* [...] *by Mr.* [Lewis] *Theobald*, 7 vols. (1733) 10
Sherlock, Thomas, *The Use and Intent of Prophecy in several Ages of the World* (1725), 4th edn (1744) 5
———, *L'usage et les fins de la prophétie dans les divers âges du monde* [...] *traduit* [...] *par Abraham Le Moine* (1729); 2nd edn (1733) and as *Discours sur l'usage et les fins* [...] *Le Moine* (Amsterdam, 1744) 5
———, *The Tryal of the Witnesses of the Resurrection of Jesus* (1729), 12th edn (1748) 5
———, *see also* Moss
Short, Thomas, *A Dissertation upon Tea* (1730) 5
Smith, John, *The Compleat Fisher*, 1st edn as *The True Art of Angling* (1696), 6th edn as *The Compleat Fisher or The True Art of Angling* [c. 1730] 5
Smith, Robert, *Harmonics, or the Philosophy of Musical Sounds* (1749) 5
Smollett, Tobias, *The Adventures of Roderick Random* (1748) 5
'Sopha, The': *see* Jolyot de Crébillon
Spectator, The (1711–12) 10
Stanhope, Philip Dormer (4th Earl of Chesterfield): *see* [Anon.], *An Apology*
Stanyan, Temple, *The Grecian History* (1707), 2nd edn, 2 vols. (1739) 5
Steele, Richard, *The Dramatick Works* [...] *I. The Conscious Lover, II. The Funeral, III. The Tender Husband, IV. The Lying Lover* ([c.1733], repr.) 5
'Stirlings Pantheon': *see* Pomey
Stow, John, *A Summarie of Englyshe Chronicles* [1565] or *A Summarie of the Chronicles of England* (1575; repr., but not in fol.) 5
Swift: *see Miscellanies*
Thomson, James, *The Castle of Indolence, an Allegorical Poem*, 2nd edn (1748) 5
'Tom Jones': *see* Fielding, Henry
'Tookes Pantheon': *see* Pomey
'Tryal of ye Witnesses': *see* Sherlock
'Universal History': *see* [Sale]
Venuti, Niccolò Marcello, *A Description of the Finest Discoveries of the Antient City of Heraclea*, trans. Wickes Skurray (1750) 5
Virgil (Publius Virgilius Maronis), *Georgicorum libri quatuor. The Georgicks of Virgil*, trans. John Martyn (1741), 2nd edn (1746) 5
Walton, Izaak, *The Compleat Angler, or Contemplative Man's Recreation* (1653); in 2 parts (1750) 5
Whitmill, Benjamin, *Kalendarium universale, or The Gardiner's Universal Calendar* (1726), 4th edn (1748) 5
[Wills, William], *A Narrative of the very extraordinary Adventures and Sufferings of Mr. William Wills, late surgeon* (1750–51) 7
Yardley, Edward, *The Good Samaritan. A Sermon preached at the Parish-Church of St. Ann, Westminster, on Tuesday, March the 7th, 1748–9* [1749] 5

Uncertain Identifications

French Gramer 5
    Either   Boyer, Abel, *The Compleat French Master* (1694), 15th edn (1748)
    Or   ————, *A New French Grammar: containing the necessary Rules for Attaining that Language* (Rotterdam, 1748)
    Or   Chambaud, Lewis, *A Grammar of the French Tongue* (1750)

Guardian^s 2 v[ols.] 5
    Either   Penton, Stephen, *The Guardian's Instruction, or, The Gentleman's Romance: Written for the Diversion and Service of the Gentry* (1688); 2nd edn as *The Guardian's Instruction* [...] *Gentry. Particularly those educated at Cambridge, and Oxford* (1697)
    Or   *The Guardian*, nos. 1–175 in two volumes (1747)
    Or   *Motto's of the Two Volumes of Guardians: in Latin and English* (1714)

Hist: Eng:^{d} Cutts & gilt 5
    Either   Thoyras, Paul Rapin de, *The History of England, written in French* [...] *translated* [...] *by* [...] *N[icolas] Tindal* (1743–7)
    Or   Lockman, John, *A New History of England, by Question and Answer. Extracted from* [...] *Mr. Rapin de Thoyras*, new edn (1749)

History of Greece Q: & Answer 5
    Either   [Anon.], *The History of Greece. By way of Question and Answer* [...] *For the Use of Schools* (1743)
    Or   Lockman, John, *A New History of Greece. By way of Question and Answer* [...] *For the Use of Schools* (1750)

Lady's Religion 5
    Either   *A Lady's Religion, in a Letter to the Honourable My Lady Howard*; 3rd edn, *To which is added a Letter to a Lady, on the Death of her Husband, by the Editor* [F. W.] (1748)
    Or   *The Religion of a Lady* (1736)

Latini Sermonis 5
    Estienne, Robert, *Thesaurus linguæ Latinæ, seu promptuarium Dictionum et loquendi formularum* [...] *Latini sermonis* [...] *ex optimis auctoribus concinnatum*, new edn by Edmund Law and others, 4 vols. (1734–5)

L[etter] to a Lady 5
    Either   [Anon.], *A Letter to a Lady, concerning the Education of Female Youth* (1749)
    Or   Bolton, Robert, *A Letter to a Lady on Card-Playing on the Lord's Day* (1748)

Life of Betterton 5
    Either   [Anon.], *An Account of the Life of that celebrated Tragedian Mr. Thomas Betterton* [...] *Interspersed with an Account of the English Theatre during his Time* (1749)
    Or   Gildon, Charles, *The Life of Mr. Thomas Betterton* (1710)

Life of Homer 10
    Either   [Blackwell, Thomas], *An Enquiry into the Life and Writings of Homer*, 4th edn (1736)
    Or   *Proofs of the Enquiry into Homer's Life and Writings*, trans. Thomas Blackwell (1747)

108 Appendix II

The Musæum 7
- Either   *Musœum Thoresbyanum, or a Catalogue of the Antiquities in the Collection of R[alph] Thoresby* (1713; [1725])
- Or   *A Catalogue of the Curious Musœum of* [...] *Mr. E[dward] Barnard* [...] *which will be sold by Auction* [1737]

New Method of Italian Tongue 5
- Either   Cori, Angelo Maria, *A New Method for the Italian Tongue; or, A Short Way to Learn It* (1723)
- Or   Lancelot, Claude, *A New Method of Learning the Italian Tongue. Translated from the French of Messieurs de Port Royal* (1750)

Œconomy of Human Life 5, 7
- Either   Dodsley, Robert, *The Œconomy of Human Life*, Part II (1750)
- And/or   Hill, John, *The Œconomy of Human Life*, Part the Second (1751)

Old Castles remarks 5
- Whatley, Stephen, *England's Gazetteer, or An Accurate Description of all the Cities, Towns, and Villages of the Kingdom* [...] *Also* [...] *the Old Military Ways, Camps, Castles, and Other Remarkable Ruins*, 3 vols. (1751)

Philips's poems 5
- Philips, Katherine, *Poems by* [...] *Mrs. Katherine Philips, the Matchless Orinda. To which is added* [...] *Corneille's Tragedies of Pompey and Horace* [...] *with several other Translations out of French* (1667; 1710)

Popes 4th & 5th Roy^{ll} pap^{r} cost 5
- Pope, Alexander, *presumably* vols. 4 and 5 from an edition of *The Works*, published in the 1730s or 1740s

Popes L.^{rs} L. P. gilt & Lrd 5
- Either   Pope, Alexander, [*Letters from Alexander Pope, Esq; and the Right Hon. the Lord Bolingbroke, to the Reverend Dr. Swift, D. S. P. D. To which is added Almahide, a Poem by Lord Bolingbroke*] (1737)
- Or   [———], *Letters to and from Alexander Pope, Esq and Others* (1748)

Religion of Nature 5
- Either   Wollaston, William, *The Religion of Nature delineated* (1722), 7th edn (1750)
- Or   ———, *A Compendious View of the Religion of Nature delineated* [an abridgment] (1726), 2nd edn (1737)
- Or   Willats, Charles, *The Religion of Nature* [...] *proved to be a mere Idol* (1744)
- Or   [Anon.], *The Religion of Nature* [...] *A Letter to the Reverend Mr. Charles Willats* (1744)

Salmon on Musick 5
- Either   Salmon, Thomas, *An Essay to the Advancement of Musick, by casting away the perplexity of Different Cliffs. And Uniting all sorts of Musick* [...] *in one Universal Character* (1672; repr.)
- Or   ———, *A Proposal to Perform Musick; Perfect and Mathematical Proportions* (1688)

Tasso Jerusalem 5
- Either   Tasso, Torquato, *Godfrey of Bulloigne, or, The Recovery of Jerusalem*, trans. Edward Fairfax (Dublin, 1726)
- Or   [Torquato] *Tasso's Jerusalem*, trans. Henry Brooke (1738)
- Or   *The Jerusalem of Torquato Tasso*, trans. Thomas Hooke (1738)

Appendix II 109

    Or   Tasso, Torquato, *Jerusalem Delivered*, trans. John Hoole (1744)
    Or   ———, *Jerusalem Delivered, or Godfrey of Bulloign*, trans. Fairfax, 4th edn (1749)
Tatlers 4 vols 5
           The Tatler, nos. 1–272 (1709–11), bound in 4 vols.
D° bound treblerola [?] wth gold 5
           The Guardian, nos. 1–175 (1747), evidently in an unusual and/or elaborate kind of binding
Two Royal African 10
           Chidley, John, *Some general Reflections [...] in Vindication of Himself from the Calumnies which the African Company have endeavoured to throw upon him in two late Papers* [1709?]
Whiston Life 2 Vols in boards 5
    Either Whiston, William, *Historical Memoirs of the Life and Writings of Dr Samuel Clarke, including certain Memoirs of Several of his Friends*, 3rd edn, 2 vols. (1748)
    Or   ———, *Memoirs of the Life and Writings of Mr. William Whiston* (1748)

Unidentified Items

Almanacks 5
an^t [or au^t] of Liturgy 5
Bibles 5
Bibles, Latin 5
Common Prayer [Books of] 5
Danoil Maps of Italy colour'd 5
Lady's Memorand[um] book 5
Life Q: Anne 5
Magaz[ine] N° 3 5
Miscell[aneous] tracts, 9 vols. 5
Pamphlets 5
Testaments 5
Testaments, Latin 5
Trade 2 vols. 5

Music

Compositions (short titles)

This list includes musical works, manuscript scores, performances and printed wordbooks. The entries in the documents may refer to the purchase, binding or performance of the compositions concerned.

[Anon.], Anthems 4
———, *Antidote Against Melancholy, An* 5
———, Concerts 9, 21
———, *Merry Man's Companion, The* 5
———, Music in the Chapel 21
———, Opera Dances 11

110 Appendix II

———, *Orazio* 5
———, *Orpheus: A Collection of* [...] *English and Scotch Songs. Vol. 1: The Linnet; vol. 2: The Robin; vol. 3: The Thrush* 5
———, *Voice of Melody* 5
Boyce, William, *The Chaplet* 5
Brooke, Henry, *Songs in Jack the Giant Queller* 5
Corelli, Arcangelo, Violin sonatas 5
———, Concertos 11
Croft, William, *Musica Sacra* 5
Handel, George Frideric, *Alexander's Feast* 21
———, Concertos 11
———, *Esther* 20
———, *Israel in Egypt* 7
———, *Joshua* 7
———, *Messiah* 10
———, Overtures 4, 11
———, *Samson* 4, 7, 11, 21
———, *Solomon* 10
———, Songs 5
———, *The Ways of Zion do mourn* 21
Hasse, Johann Adolf, *Venetian Ballads* 5
Pescetti, Giovanni Battista, *Demetrius* 11
Temple of Apollo, Society of the, *Comic Tunes in Queen Mab* 7

Instruments (including strings, bows, etc.)

Bell 9
Cello 3, 12, 13
Double bass 12
Harpsichord 6
Viola 12
Violin 3, 12, 13
'Whole band' 21

Plays

This is an alphabetical list of the individual plays that are mentioned in the documents. The dates in parenthesis are those of first performance or publication. The entries in the documents may relate to the purchase, binding (with or without interleaving) or staging of the plays. For collected editions of dramatic works by, for example, Congreve and Steele see above, 'Books'.

Athelwold, Aaron Hill (1731) 2, 4
Cobler of Preston, The, Christopher Bullock or Charles Johnson (1716) 7
Constant Couple, The, or A Trip to the Jubilee, George Farquhar (1700) 5
Double Discovery: see *Spanish Fryar*
Double Falsehood, or The Distressed Lovers, Lewis Theobald (1728) 2, 4, 5

Drummer, The, or The Haunted House, Joseph Addison (1715) 7
Edward and Eleonora, James Thomson (1739) 7
Fair Penitent, The, Nicholas Rowe (1703) 7
False Marriage 4
Fatal Marriage, The, or The Innocent Adultery, Thomas Southerne (1694) 4, 10
Forc'd Marriage, The, Aphra Behn (1670) 4 (Commentary)
Funeral, The, or Grief a-la-mode, Richard Steele (1701) 4
Hamlet, William Shakespeare 4
Henry IV Part I, William Shakespeare 2, 4, 17[a], 17[b]
Henry IV Part II, William Shakespeare 7
Jane Shore, Nicholas Rowe (1714) 2, 4, 7
King Lear, William Shakespeare 4
Merope, Aaron Hill (1749) 10
Merry Wives of Windsor, The, William Shakespeare 7
Mock Marriage, The, Thomas Scott (?1695) 4 (Commentary)
Orphan, The, or The Unhappy Marriage, Thomas Otway (1680) 4
Othello, William Shakespeare 7
Regicide, The, or James the First of Scotland, Tobias Smollett (1749) 5
Richard the Third, William Shakespeare 7
Spanish Fryar, The, or The Double Discovery, John Dryden (1681) 7
Trip to the Jubilee: see *Constant Couple*
[*Twelfth Night*], William Shakespeare 17[a]
Venice Preserv'd, Thomas Otway (1682) 5, 7
Walking Statue, The, or The Devil in the Wine-cellar, Aaron Hill (1709) 7

Theatre

Costumes 17[a], 17[b]
Curtains 17[a], 17[b]
Properties 2, 17[a], 17[b]
Scenery 1, 2, 15[a], 15[b], 16, 17[a], 17[b]
Soundboard 17[b]
Stages 2 (including model), 8, 15[b], 16, 17[b]

Bibliography

A list of literary works (i.e., not music) mentioned in notes or commentaries in chapters or appendices.

Manuscript

London, British Library, Add. MS 23724: Arthur Pond, 'Journal of Receipts & Expenses from 1734–1750'
British Library, Add. MS 29601: Mrs Margret Smith, letters

Online

British Newspaper Archive (British Library)
A Cambridge Alumni Database (ACAD)
Dataset of Subscribers to Eighteenth-Century Music Publications in Britain and Ireland, by Simon D. I. Fleming and Martin Perkins
Historical Manuscripts Commission, GB-0056-DE3214: Summary Report on the Estate and Family Papers, 12th–20th century, of the Noel family, Earls of Gainsborough, by J. Gurney and R. Olney
Oxford Dictionary of National Biography (ODNB) online
Répertoire International des Sources Musicales (RISM) online
Seventeenth and Eighteenth Century Burney Newspapers Collection

Printed

Abbot, Djilda and Ephraim Segerman, 'Gut Strings', *Early Music*, 4 (1976), 430–37
Alotaibi, Naseem, 'Lewis Theobald's *Double Falsehood*: The Authorship Question Reconsidered', Ph.D. dissertation (University of Liverpool, 2016)
Baker, Malcolm, *The Marble Index: Roubiliac and Sculptural Portraiture in Eighteenth-Century Britain* (New Haven: Yale University Press, 2014)
———, 'Sculpting Reputation: A Terracotta Bust of Senesino by Roubiliac', *Metropolitan Museum Journal*, 57 (2022), 25–40
Brewer, John, *The Pleasures of the Imagination: English Culture in the Eighteenth Century* (Abingdon: Routledge, 2013)

Browne, Richard, *A Mechanical Essay on Singing, Musick and Dancing. Containing their Uses and Abuses; and Demonstrating by Clear and Evident Reasons, the Alterations they produce in the Human Body* (London: J. Pemberton, 1727)
——, *Medicina Musica: or, A Mechanical Essay on the Effects of Singing, Musick, and Dancing, on Human Bodies. Revis'd and corrected. To which is annex'd A New Essay on the Nature and Cure of the Spleen and Vapours* (London: John Cooke, 1729)
Burney, Charles, *A General History of Music from the Earliest Ages to the Present Period*, ed. Frank Mercer, 2 vols. (London: G. T. Foulis, 1935)
Burrows, Donald, 'Do We Need "John"?', *Handel Institute Newsletter*, 30 (2019), 3
Burrows, Donald and Rosemary Dunhill, *Music and Theatre in Handel's World: The Family Papers of James Harris 1732–1780* (New York: Oxford University Press, 2002)
The Cambridge Companion to the Violin, ed. Robin Stowell (Cambridge: Cambridge University Press, 2011)
Cantor, Leonard and Anthony Squires, *The Historic Parks and Gardens of Leicestershire and Rutland* (Newton Linford: Kairos Press, 1997)
A Catalogue of Original Pictures lately consigned from Abroad, Out of the Galleries of the Two Brothers the Barons of Vicq, at Brussels and Brughes [...] To be sold by Auction, by Mr. Lambe, at his Great Auction Room in Pall Mall [...] (London: s. n. 1749)
Clark, Jenny, 'Family Annals: The Exton Manuscripts', *Rutland Record*, 13 (1993), 118–24
——, 'Exton and the Noel Family', *Rutland Record*, 19 (1999), 382–99
The Clergyman's Intelligencer: or A Compleat Alphabetical List of all the Patrons in England and Wales, with the Dignities, Livings, and Benefices in their Gift; and their Valuations Annex'd (London: J. and P. Knapton and others, 1745)
Coke, David and Alan Borg, *Vauxhall Gardens: A History* (New Haven: Yale University Press, 2011)
Crosby, Brian, 'Private Concerts on Land and Water: The Musical Activities of the Sharp Family, c. 1750–c. 1790', *Royal Musical Association Research Chronicle*, 34 (2001), 1–118
Crosse, John, *An Account of the Grand Musical Festival, held in September, 1823, in the Cathedral Church of York [...] To which is prefixed, A Sketch of the Rise and Progress of Musical Festivals in Great Britain; with Biographical and Historical Notes* (New York: John Wolstenholme, 1825)
Duncan, Cheryll, *Felice Giardini and Professional Music Culture in Mid-Eighteenth-Century London* (Royal Musical Association Monographs 35) (Abingdon: Routledge, 2020)
Educating the Child in Enlightenment Britain: Beliefs, Cultures, Practices, ed. Mary Hilton and Jill Shefrin (Farnham: Ashgate, 2009)
The Eighteenth Century (Blackwell History of Music in Britain, 4), ed. H. Diack Johnstone and Roger Fiske (Oxford: Blackwell, 1990)
Fiske, Roger, *English Theatre Music in the Eighteenth Century*, 2nd edn (Oxford: Oxford University Press, 1986)
Fleming, Simon D. I., 'The Musical Activities of the Spalding Gentlemen's Society', *Royal Musical Association Research Chronicle*, 48 (2017), 65–90
Fletcher, Anthony, *Growing up in England: The Experience of Childhood 1600–1914* (New Haven: Yale University Press, 2008)

Frew, Catherine and Arnold Myers, 'Sir Samuel Hellier's "Musicall Instruments"', *Galpin Society Journal*, 56 (2003), 6–26 and 186–9

Gardner, Matthew, *Handel and Maurice Greene's Circle at the Apollo Academy* (Göttingen: V&R Unipress, 2008)

George Frideric Handel: Collected Documents, ed. Donald Burrows, Helen Coffey, John Greenacombe and Anthony Hicks, 6 vols. (Cambridge: Cambridge University Press, 2013–)

Gibbons, Alicia Clair and George N. Heller, 'Music Therapy in Handel's England: Browne's *Medicina Musica* (1729)', *College Music Symposium*, 25 (1985), 59–72

Girouard, Mark, *Life in the English Country House* (New Haven: Yale University Press, 1978)

Grant, Hester, *The Good Sharps: The Eighteenth-Century Family that Changed Britain* (London: Vintage, 2021)

Handel, George Frideric, *Music for 'Comus'*, ed. Colin Timms and Anthony Hicks (London: Acca Music, 1977)

Handel: A Celebration of his Life and Times, 1685–1759, ed. Jacob Simon (London: National Portrait Gallery, 1985)

Handel, George Frideric and Thomas Augustine Arne, *Comus*, ed. Colin Timms (London: Novello, 2016)

Hankins, Thomas L. and Robert J. Silverman, *Instruments and Imagination* (Princeton: Princeton University Press, 1995)

Harris, Ellen T., *George Frideric Handel: A Life with Friends* (New York: Norton, 2014)

Hayes, John, 'Introduction', in *Polite Society* (q.v.)

A History of the County of Rutland, ed. William Page, 2 vols. (London: Constable, 1908, and St Catherine Press, 1935)

Hughes, John, *Poems on Several Occasions: with some Select Essays in Prose [...] Adorn'd with Sculptures*, 2 vols. (London: J. Tonson and J. Watts, 1735)

Hunter, David, 'Handel at Exton, Rutland', *Handel Institute Newsletter*, 25/1 (2014), 6–7

———, *The Lives of George Frideric Handel* (Woodbridge: Boydell, 2015)

Johan Zoffany RA: Society Observed, ed. Martin Postle (New Haven: Yale University Press, 2011)

Johnstone, H. Diack, 'John Blathwayt: A Musical British Teenager on the Grand Tour', *The Musical Times*, 162 (Summer 2021), 27–47

Kent's Directory for the Year 1763 (London: Henry Kent, 1763)

Kidson, Frank, 'James Oswald, Dr. Burney, and "The Temple of Apollo"', *The Musical Antiquary*, 2 (1910–11), 34–41

Ledsham, Ian, *A Catalogue of the Shaw-Hellier Collection in the Music Library, Barber Institute of Fine Arts, the University of Birmingham* (Aldershot: Ashgate, 1999)

Leppert, Richard, *Music and Image: Domesticity, Ideology and Socio-Cultural Formation in Eighteenth-Century England*, paperback edn (Cambridge: Cambridge University Press, 1993)

Lippincott, Louise, *Selling Art in Georgian London: The Rise of Arthur Pond* (London: Yale University Press, 1983)

Lyric Repository: A Collection of Original, Ancient, & Modern Songs, Duets, Catches, Glees & Cantat: Selected for their Poetical and Literary Merit, vol. 1 (London: J. French, 1787)

Bibliography 115

Martyn, Thomas, *The English Connoisseur: containing an Account of* [...] *Painting, Sculpture, &c. in the Palaces and Seats of the Nobility and Principal Gentry of England (1766)*, 2nd edn (Dublin: T. and J. Whitehouse, 1767)

Marx, Hans Joachim, *Die Überlieferung der Werke Arcangelo Corellis: Catalogue raisonnée* (Cologne: Arno Volk-Hans Gerig, 1980)

——, *'By Heaven Inspired': Die Bildnisse von Georg Friedrich Händel* (Lilienthal: Laaber, 2021)

Matthews, Betty, 'Unpublished Letters concerning Handel', *Music & Letters*, 40 (1959), 261–8

Memoirs of Doctor Burney, arranged from his Own Manuscripts, from Family Papers, and from Personal Recollections, by Madame d'Arblay [Fanny Burney], 3 vols. (London: Edward Moxon, 1832)

McGeary, Thomas, 'Handel as Art Collector: Art, Connoisseurship and Taste in Hanoverian Britain', *Early Music*, 37 (2009), 533–74

Mortimer, Thomas, *The Universal Director; or, The Nobleman and Gentleman's True Guide to the Masters and Professors of the Liberal and Polite Arts and Sciences and of the Mechanic Arts, Manufactures, and Trades, established in London and Westminster, and their Environs*, 2 vols. (London: J. Coote, 1763)

Music by Subscription: Composers and their Networks in the British Music Publishing Trade, 1676–1820, ed. Simon D. I. Fleming and Martin Perkins (London: Routledge, 2021)

Music in the British Provinces 1690–1914, ed. Rachel Cowgill and Peter Holman (Aldershot: Ashgate, 2007)

The New Grove Dictionary of Music and Musicians, 2nd edn, ed. Stanley Sadie and John Tyrrell, 29 vols. (London: Macmillan, 2001)

Nisser, Wilhelm, *Michael Dahl and the Contemporary Swedish School of Painting* (Uppsala: Almqvist & Wiksell, 1927)

Noel, Emilia F., *Some Letters and Records of the Noel Family* (London: St Catherine Press, 1910)

Noel, Gerard, *Sir Gerard Noel MP and the Noels of Chipping Campden and Exton* (Chipping Campden: Campden and District Historical and Archaeological Society, 2004)

Perkins, Martin, 'Music in Country Houses of the English Midlands, 1750–1810', 2 vols., Ph.D. dissertation (Birmingham City University, 2020/21)

Pevsner, Nikolaus, *Leicestershire and Rutland*, 2nd edn, revised Elizabeth Williamson with Geoffrey K. Brandwood (Harmondsworth: Penguin, 1984)

Polite Society by Arthur Devis (1712–1787): Portraits of the English Country Gentleman and his Family, ed. Michael Cross (Preston: Harris Museum and Art Gallery, 1983)

Purser, John, *Scotland's Music: A History of the Traditional and Classical Music of Scotland from the Earliest Times to the Present Day* (Edinburgh: Mainstream, 1992)

Revisiting Shakespeare's Lost Play: 'Cardenio/Double Falsehood' in the Eighteenth Century, ed. Deborah C. Payne (Cham: Palgrave Macmillan, 2016)

Roberts, John H., 'The Composition of Handel's *Esther*, 1718–1720', *Händel-Jahrbuch*, 55 (2009), 353–90

Rosenfeld, Sybil, *Temples of Thespis: Some Private Theatres and Theatricals in England and Wales, 1700–1820* (London: Society for Theatre Research, 1978)

Schnapper, Edith B., *The British Union-Catalogue of Early Music printed before the Year 1801*, 2 vols. (London: Butterworths Scientific Publications, 1957)

Scholes, Percy A., *The Great Dr. Burney: His Life – His Travels – His Works – His Family and his Friends*, 2 vols. (London: Oxford University Press, 1948)

A Select Collection of Poems: with Notes Biographical and Historical, vol. 4 (London: J. Nichols, 1780)

Settle, Elkanah, *Thalia lacrimans: A Funeral Poem to the Memory of the Right Honourable Baptist Earl of Gainsborough* (London: The Author, 1714)

Skynner, John, *A Sermon preach'd at the Funeral of Baptist Earl of Gainsborough, April 18, 1751* (London: R. Dodsley, [1751])

Smart, Thomas William Wake, *A Chronology of Cranborne, being an Account of the ancient Town, Lordship, and Chase of Cranborne in the County of Dorset* (London: Nichols and Sons, and Others, 1841)

Smith, James Edward, *English Botany*, 36 vols. (London: The Author, 1790–1814)

Smith, Ruth, 'The Achievements of Charles Jennens (1700–1773)', *Music & Letters*, 70 (1989), 161–90

———, *Charles Jennens: The Man Behind Handel's Messiah* (London: Handel House Trust and Gerald Coke Handel Foundation, 2012)

Smith, William C. and Charles Humphries, *A Bibliography of the Musical Works published by the firm of John Walsh during the Years 1726–1766* (London: The Bibliographical Society,1968)

———, *Handel: A Descriptive Catalogue of the Early Editions*, 2nd edn with supplement (Oxford: Basil Blackwell, 1970)

Stourton, James and Charles Sebag-Montefiore, *The British as Art Collectors: From the Tudors to the Present* (London: Scala, 2012)

Sumner, Brenda, 'Charles Jennens' Piano and Music Room', *Handel Institute Newsletter*, 22/2 (2011), 1–3

Symes, Michael, *The English Landscape Garden: A Survey* (Swindon: Historic England, 2019)

Talbot, Michael, 'From Giovanni Stefano Carbonelli to John Stephen Carbonell: A Violinist turned Vintner in Handel's London', *Göttinger Händel-Beiträge*, 14 (2012), 265–99

Taylor, Carole, 'John (Manners), 3rd Duke of Rutland: British Art Collector', *Journal of the History of Collections*, 29/2 (2017), 237–50

Theobald, Lewis, *Double Falshood; or, The Distrest Lovers*, 2nd edn (London: John Watts, 1728)

———, *Double Falsehood*, ed. Brean Hammond (London: Arden Shakespeare, 2010)

Timms, Colin, 'Lord Gainsborough buys a Bust of Handel from Roubiliac', *Händel-Jahrbuch*, 67 (2021), 59–71

———, 'Handel and *Comus* at Exton', in *New Perspectives on Handel's Music: Essays in Honour of Donald Burrows*, ed. David Vickers (Woodbridge: Boydell, 2022), 243–66

———, 'Handel Translators: Humphreys, Oldmixon and Anonymous', *Händel-Jahrbuch*, 70 (2024)

Treadwell, Penelope, *Johan Zoffany: Artist and Adventurer* (London: Paul Holberton, 2009)

Turner, Roger, *Capability Brown and the Eighteenth-Century English Landscape Garden* (London: Weidenfeld & Nicolson, 1985)

Bibliography 117

Venn, John, *Alumni Cantabrigiensis: A Biographical List of all known Students, Graduates and Holders of Office at the University of Cambridge, from the Earliest Times to 1900, vol. 1: From the Earliest Times to 1751* (Cambridge: Cambridge University Press, 2011)

Vickery, Amanda, *The Gentleman's Daughter: Women's Lives in Georgian England* (New Haven: Yale University Press, 1998)

Webster, Mary, *Johan Zoffany, 1733–1810* (New Haven: Yale University Press, 2011)

Young, Percy, 'The Shaw-Hellier Collection', in *Handel Collections and their History*, ed. Terence Best (Oxford: Clarendon Press, 1993), 158–70

Zimmerman, Franklin B., *Henry Purcell, 1659–1695: An Analytical Catalogue of his Music* (London: Macmillan, 1963)

Index

This is an index to the Introduction, the Chapters and Appendix I; Appendix II is indexed separately on pp. 99–111. With regard to names that constantly recur throughout the book (e.g., Exton and Gainsborough), only important references are indexed. Titled individuals are entered under their title but with a cross-reference from their family name. Entries relating to tables are in bold type, those to figures in italic.

Abel, Carl Friedrich (composer) 56
Abingdon (Willoughby Bertie), 4th Earl of 56
Addison, Joseph (writer, playwright) 44
Æsop 30
Aglionby, William (art historian) 30
Agnese (painter) 10, 11
Alberti (painter) 10, 11
Albinus, Bernhard Siegfried (anatomist) 29
Alcoforado, Francisco (explorer, writer) 29
Aler, Paul 31 (author)
Alfred, The Masque in 35
Alken, Sefferin (carver) 10, 11
Alla maestà di Giorgio Rè (Ariosti) 13, 62
Amphitheatria, or Majesty in Liquor 3n6
Anacreon 13, 24n51, 63
Annet, Peter (philosopher) 29
Anson, George (admiral, politician) 11, 29
Antidote against Melancholy, An 34
Anville, Jean Baptiste Bourguignon d' (cartographer) 29
Arblay, Madame d' *see* Burney, Fanny

Arbuthnot, John (physician, satirist) 29
Ariosti, Attilio (composer) 13, 62, 63
Arne, Thomas Augustine (composer) 1, 41, 57
Athelwold (Hill) 45, 46
Atterbury, Francis (bishop, politician) 29
Aubourn (Lincs.) 5

Bach, John Christian (composer) 56
Badeslade, Thomas (topographical draughtsman) *8*
band 33, 40 *see also* orchestra
Banier, Antoine (historian) 30, 31
Baptista (painter) 10, 11
Barber, Mary (poet) 63
Bath, Lady (wife of William Pulteney, 1st Earl of Bath) 42
Belvoir Castle 10, 20–21, 34
Berrey, Kell (carpenter) 43
Betterton, Thomas (actor, theatre manager) 30
Bickham, George (engraver) 13, 63
Birch, Thomas (historian) 11
Blackheath 5, 9
Blackwell, Thomas (historian) 30
Blathwait (Blathwayt), W. 50
Blavet, Michel (composer) 35

Index

Boccaccio, Giovanni (poet) 12, 61
Bolingbroke *see* St John
Bononcini, Giovanni (composer) 13, 62, 63
Bonus, James (picture restorer) 11
books: Gainsborough's expenditure on **27–8**; overview by subject **28**; books by French authors 31; educational 31
books on: gardening 29; geography 29; history 29–30; language 31; law 29; literature 30; medicine 29; music 30; nature 29; philosophy 29; politics 29; religion 29; visual arts 30
Bowen, Emanuel (engraver) 29
Bower, Archibald (historian) 62
Boyce, William (composer): sonatas 13, 63; *The Chaplet* 34
Brooke House 4, 13
Brooks, James (composer) 55
Brown, John 46
Brown, Lancelot ('Capability'; landscape designer) 8–9
Browne, Richard (author) 15, *16*, 18, 29, 61
Bullock, Christopher (dramatist) 44
Burnet, Gilbert (historian, philosopher) 62
Burney, Charles (composer, music historian) 35, 36
Burney, Fanny (novelist) 36

Cæsar, Julius 30
Cambridge: King's College 1; St John's College 4, 11
Campbel, Duncan (soothsayer) 61
Campden (Baptist Noel), Viscount 39, 50, 54
Cantrell, Mary (wife of Rev. William Cantrell) 18
Carbonelli, Giovanni Stefano (violinist, composer) 34
carpentry 26, 42–3
Castiglione, Baldassar (diplomat, author) 12, 61
Cervantes, Miguel de (writer) 46
Chaplet, The (Boyce) 34

Chapman, Elizabeth *see* Gainsborough, Countess of
Chapman, Mr 38
Cheny, John (writer on horse racing) 61
Chesterfield (Philip Stanhope), 4th Earl of 29
Chipping Campden 4, 10
Christian, Benjamin (binder) 36, 37, 39, 41, 45, 50
Cibber, Colley (actor) 30
Cicero, Marcus Tullius 30
Cleland, John (novelist) 30
Clingworth, Oliver (needleworker: scenery) 43
Cobham (Richard Temple), 1st Viscount 8–9
Cobler of Preston, The (Bullock or Johnson) 44
Comus see Arne, Dalton, Handel works, Milton
concerts 2, 33, 39, 40, 56
Congreve, William (playwright) 30
Constant Couple, The, or A Trip to the Jubilee (Farquhar) 44
Cooke, John (bookseller, publisher) 15–*16*, 27, 34, 37–8, 44, 50
Cooper, Anthony Ashley *see* Shaftesbury
Corelli, Arcangelo (composer): concertos 36, 40; sonatas 34, 40
Cornwall, Henry (sea captain) 63
Croft, William (composer) 34, 41
Crosse, John (antiquary) 56–7
Cumbrey, H. 50

Dalton, John (author) 1, 57
dance(s) 15, *16*–17, 36–7, 40, 50
Davys, Mary (novelist, playwright) 61
De Curli (writer) 31
Defoe, Daniel (writer) 30
Demetrius (Pescetti) 37
Despairing Shepherd, The (Burney) 35
Disney, Colonel 9
Dothel Figlio 36
Double Discovery, see Spanish Fryar, The

Double Falsehood (Theobald) 44,
   45, 46–9, 50, 58; music in 47–9
drawing(s) 10, 31, 39
Drummer, The (Addison) 44, 45
Dryden, John (poet, critic) 30, 45
Du Pin, Louis Ellies (historian) 29, 31
Dubos, Jean-Baptiste (author) 30, 31

Edward and Eleonora
   (Thomson) 44
Edwards, George (naturalist) 29
Edwards, Gerard Anne, 5
Edwards, Gerard Noel 5
Edwards, Thomas (critic, poet) 30
Egerton (Sir Horatio Mann), 2nd
   Baronet of 5
Eton College 4, 30
Evans, George, 3rd Baron Carbery 5
Exton 1, 4, 5; academy of music 56
Exton estate 2, 6–9, 54; bowling
   41, 50, 59; church or chapel 13,
   40–41, 42, 54; Fort Henry
   54; gardens 2, 6–9, 19, 40,
   41–2, 54
Exton Hall 1–2, 4, 10, 11–12, 19,
   42–4, 55–6; music rooms 32–3
Eyre, Joseph (composer) 55

Faber, John, junior (engraver) 6
Fair Penitent, The (Rowe) 44
Fancort, John (carpenter) 42–3
Fancort, Will (carpenter) 42–3
Farquhar, George (dramatist) 44
Festing, Michael Christian 13, *14*,
   24n50, 33–4, 40, 63
Fielding, Henry (novelist) 30
fireworks 1, 2
Fletcher, John (playwright) 46
Florus, Annæus Lucius (historian)
   29, 31
Funeral, The, or Grief a-la-mode
   (Steele) 45

Gainsborough (Baptist Noel), 3rd
   Earl of 4, 21n4
Gainsborough (Baptist Noel), 4th
   Earl of: ancestors 4, 6, 22n13; life
   4–12, 54, 55–6, 57–9; daughters
   5–6, 17, 38, 39–40, 47; character
   31–2; houses in London 5, 9
Gainsborough (Baptist Noel), 4th
   Earl of, interests: books 27–32,
   61–2; education 16–17, 31,
   58, 62; horses 2, 7, 8, 10, 12,
   23n47; music 13–21, 32–41;
   62–3; painting 12, 18;
   performance 1, 18, 46, 50, 57, 58;
   poetry 12, 18–21; *see also* plays,
   theatre
Gainsborough (Baptist Noel), 5th
   Earl of 5, 54, 56
Gainsborough (Edward Noel), 1st
   Earl of 4
Gainsborough (Henry Noel), 6th
   Earl of 5, 54–5, 56
Gainsborough (Dorothy Manners),
   dowager countess of 4, 13, 63
Gainsborough (Elizabeth *née*
   Chapman), Countess of 4–6, 12,
   13, 22n21, 31, 40, 63
Gann, Phillip (carpenter) 42, 43
Garrick, David (actor) 35
Gay, John (poet, dramatist) 35
Gee, Philippa 1
Geminiani, Francesco
   (composer) 35
Geneva 5
Giardini, Felice (violinist,
   composer) 33
Gilpin, William (clergyman, author)
   8, 29
Godwin, Francis (author) 30
Goodwin, Samuel (scene painter)
   42, 45
Gopsall Hall 32
Gouge, Mr. (composer) 47, *48*,
   53n45
Goupy, Joseph (engraver,
   painter) 10
Greene, Maurice (composer) 35
Greenwich 5
Griffier, Jan, the Elder (painter) 10
Grundy, John (engineer) 32
Guest, Jane Mary (composer) 55
Guthrie, William (historian) 30
Gwynn, John (architect) 31

Halifax (George Savile), 1st Marquis of 30
Hamilton, Gawen (painter) 6
Hamlet (Shakespeare) 45, 50
Handel, George Frideric 1–2, 10, 13, 17–18, 36–9, 41, 49, 63
Handel works: *Alcina* 41; *Alexander's Feast* 40, 58, 63; *L'Allegro, il Penseroso ed il Moderato* 41; *Athalia* 29; *Belshazzar* 41; *Comus* 1–2, 5–6, 17, 18, 33, 39, 41–2, 57–8; concertos 36; *Deborah* 1, 17–18, 24n61, 29, 41, 58; *Esther* 29, 41; *Flavio* 41; *Israel in Egypt* 37, 41; *Joseph and his Brethren* 17, 18; *Joshua* 37, 41; *Messiah* 18; overtures 36; *Samson* 17, 40, 41, 58; *Saul* 17; *Semele* 17; *Solomon* 18, 27, 47–9; songs 37; *Susanna* 17; *Theodora* 17; *Ways of Zion do mourn, The* 40, 41, 58
Harington, James, Sir 4
Harington, Mabel 4
Harris, James (author) 17, 57
Harris, John (engraver) 6–8
Harris, Thomas (lawyer, brother of James) 17
Hartley, David (philosopher) 29
Hasse, Johann Adolf (composer) 37
Hatchett, William (translator) 31
Hebden, John (composer) 13, 38, 59n14, 63
Heighington, Musgrave (composer): *Six Select Odes* 13, 24n51, 63; Anniversary Ode 56–7
Hellier, Samuel (musical amateur) 57
Henesy, J. (painter) 6–7
Henry IV Part I (Shakespeare) 45, 49, 54, 58
Henry IV Part II (Shakespeare) 44, 45
Herodian 29
Herring, Anthony (carpenter) 42
Hicks, Baptist, Sir (merchant) 4
Hicks, Juliana (daughter of Sir Baptist Hicks) 4

Hill, Aaron (playwright, poet) 44, 45, 46
Hill, John (author) 30
Hobs, John (carpenter) 43
Hogarth, William (painter, engraver) 6
Holinshed, Raphael (chronicler) 30
Holt, John (critic) 30
Homer 12, 30, 61
Horace (Quintus Horatius Flaccus), 13, 24n51, 30, 63
Horizonti (painter) 10
Horsfield 10
Houbraken, Jacobus (engraver) 12
Hughes, John (poet) 30
Humphreys, Samuel (translator) 29, 31, 51n6
Hysing, Hans (painter) 6

illuminations 2
Isham, Edmund, Sir (politician) 1
Italy 5

Jane Shore (Rowe) 45, 46
Jemmat, Catherine (author) 55
Jennens, Charles (librettist) 10, 32, 56
Johnson, Charles (playwright) 44
Jolyot de Crébillon, Claude Prosper (poet, tragedian) 31
Jommelli, Niccolò (composer) 35
Jones, John (clergyman) 29

Keach, Benjamin (preacher, author) 31
Ketton (Rutland) 5
King Lear (Shakespeare) 44, 45
Knapton, George (painter) 11
Knapton, John and Paul (publishers) 11

La Condamine, Charles-Marie de (explorer) 29, 31
La Morlière, Charles-Jacques-Louis-Auguste Rochette de (playwright) 31
La Rochefoucauld, François, Duc de (author) 29, 31

Index

Lambe, Aaron (auctioneer) 11
Lambert, Marchioness de *see*
  Marguenat de Courcelles
Lancaster, Nathaniel (author) 30
Leapor, Mary (poet) 62
Legg, William (architect) 54
Lely, Peter (painter) 10
Lens, Bernard (artist) 30, 31
Lesage (or Le Sage), Alain-René
  (novelist, playwright) 31
Linnean Society 54, 55
Littleton, Edward (preacher) 29
Lobb, Theophilus (physician) 29
London 11, 18, 27, 33–4, 36,
  40, 50n2; Cavendish Square
  9; Chandos Street 9; Covent
  Garden theatre 1, 18; Drury
  Lane theare 1, 34, 46; Pall Mall
  9, 11; Ranelagh Gardens 34;
  Vauxhall Gardens 40, 41; *see
  also* Blackheath, Greenwich,
  Marylebone, Westminster
Long, Samuel (conposer) 55
Low, John (needleworker: scenery) 43
Lowe, William (cabinet maker) 33

Maclean, Charles (composer) 13, 63
Mann, Horatio *see* Egerton
Manners, Dorothy *see* Gainsborough
Manners, John *see* Rutland
Manners, Sherard 2
Marchand (or Marchant), F.
  (composer) *19*–20, 25n67
Marguenat de Courcelles, Anne
  Thérèse de, Marchioness de
  Lambert 31, 62, 63
Martyn, Benjamin (writer) 18, 41–2
Marylebone 5
Mason, James (engraver) *8*–*9*
Merope (Hill) 44
Merry Man's Companion, The 34
Merry Wives of Windsor, The
  (Shakespeare) 44, 45
Miller, Philip (botanist, gardener) 29
Milton, John (poet) 17, 41; *Comus*
  1, 57–8
Molière (Jean-Baptiste Poquelin;
  playwright) 31

Montesquieu, Charles-Louis de
  Secondat, Baron de (philosopher)
  29, 31
Muller, John (author) 29
music: benefits of 16–17; binding
  37–8; copying 38–9; performance
  2, 39–41, 56–7; 58;
  purchase 34–7
music rooms *see* Exton Hall
Musica Sacra (Croft) 34, 41
Musical Entertainer, The (Bickham)
  13, 63
musical instruments: Aeolian harp
  35; bell(s) 39, 47; (double) bass
  13; flute 35, 36; harpsichord
  34, 39–40; organ 13; violin 13,
  33–4, 35, 36; viola d'amore 13;
  violoncello 13, 33; virginals 13;
  wind 13
musical works: aria 13; anthem
  34; ballad 37; cantata 35, 62;
  concerto 36, 63; dance 36–7, 40;
  duet 35; hymn 34; lesson 62; ode
  13, 24n51, 56–7, 63; opera 13,
  34, 37, 40, 63; oratorio 2, 18, 41;
  overture 36; psalm tune 34; solo
  36, 63, 64; sonata 35, 36, 62, 63;
  song 34, 35, 40, 62, 63; *see also*
  Boyce, Festing, Gouge, Handel,
  Hebden, Heighington, Marchand,
  Oswald, Pescetti, Sammartini

Nepos, Cornelius (biographer) 30
Nevile, Christopher 5
Newbould, John (needleworker:
  costumes, scenery) 42, 43–4, 45, 46
Noel, Anne 5, 54, 56
Noel, Baptist (1685–1714) *see*
  Gainsborough, 3rd Earl of
Noel, Baptist (1708–51) *see*
  Gainsborough, 4th Earl of
Noel, Baptist (1740–59) *see*
  Campden, Viscount *and*
  Gainsborough, 5th Earl of
Noel, Catharine-Susanna 5
Noel, Catherine 6, 17, 21n10
Noel, Edward, Sir *see*
  Gainsborough, 1st Earl of

Noel, Elizabeth 5, 54
Noel family: and drama 46, 50;
 and music 13, 17, 18, 34, 47,
 57; family papers 2, 3n8, 11, 26,
 55–6, 57; paintings 6, 11, 22n13,
 22n15, 32
Noel, Henry *see* Gainsborough, 6th
 Earl of
Noel, James 6, 41, 46, 57
Noel, Jane 5, 46
Noel, Juliana 5, 45, 46
Noel, Lucy 5
Noel, Mary (1744–1820) 5,
 54, 56
Noel, Miss (in 1775) 55
Noel, Mrs (in 1748) 42
Noel, Penelope 5, 18
Noel, Sophia 5, 54
Noel, Susanna *see* Shaftesbury
Noel, Thomas 17, 54
Noel, William 56, 59n14
Nollekens, Joseph (sculptor) 54
North Luffenham (Rutland) 5, 56

Oakham 15
Orazio (opera) 34
orchestra 33, 51n17; *see also* band
*Orphan, The, or The Unhappy
 Marriage* (Otway), 45, 50
Orpheus: A Collection of [...]
 Songs 34
Oswald, James (composer,
 publisher) 35–6
Othello (Shakespeare), 44, 45
Otway, Thomas (dramatist) 45, 50
Oudart Feudrix de Bréquigny, Louis
 Georges (historian) 30, 31
Oughton, Thomas (lawyer) 62
Ovid (Publius Ovidius Naso) 30
Oxford 57; Holywell music room
 32–3

painting(s) 6–7, 10–11, 39
Panini, Giovanni Paolo (painter,
 architect) 10
paper 38–9
parchment 38
Parry, John (composer) 55

Pascal, Blaise (physicist, writer) 31
Peck, Frances (clergyman) 62
Pescetti, Giovanni Battista
 (composer) 37
picture(s) *see* painting(s)
Philips, Charles (painter) 6
Pickwell (Leics.) 10
Pilkington, Laetitia (poet) 30
Pindar 30
Pixell, John (composer) 55
Plautus, Titus Maccius 62, 64
plays 2, 43–4; binding 45;
 interleaving 45; productions at
 Exton 45–50, 57, 58; repertory
 at Exton 44–5; *see also* Dryden,
 Hill (Aaron), Otway, Rowe,
 Shakespeare, Steele,
 Theobald, Thomson
Pluche, Antoine-Noël (priest) 29, 31
poetry 30, 35, 50
Pomey, François-Antoine (historian,
 philologist) 30, 31
Pond, Arthur (artist) 11
Pope, Alexander (poet, satirist) 30
Pote, Joseph (bookseller, publisher)
 30, 31
Pozzo, Andrea (painter, architect) 30
prints 10, 11

Queen Mab, The Comic Tunes in
 34–5

Rameau, Jean-Philippe
 (composer) 35
Randall, John (organist) 1
Randall, William (publisher) 36
Ranelagh Gardens 34
*Regicide, The, or James the First of
 Scotland* (Smollett) 44
Reid, John (composer) 36
Ribadeneyra, Antonio de Solis y
 (historian, playwright) 30
Richard the Third (Shakespeare) 44
Richardson, Samuel (writer) 30
Ridlington (Rutland) 10
Rogers, Andrew (stationer) 27,
 34–5, 44, 45
Rolli, Paolo (poet) 12

Rollin, Charles (historian) 29
Roque, John (cartographer) 62
Roubiliac, Louis-François (sculptor) 58
Rowe, Nicholas (playwright, actor) 44, 45, 46
Rowning, John (philosopher) 29
Royal Academy of Music 13
Rutherforth, Thomas (theologian, scientist) 62
Rutland (John Manners), 3rd Duke of 10, 20–21, 34

St John, Henry, Viscount Bolingbroke 29
Sale, George (historian) 30
Salmon, Thomas (historian) 30
Sammartini, Giuseppe (composer) 35, 36
Savage, Richard (poet) 61, 63
Savile, George *see* Halifax
Scheemakers, Peter (sculptor) 10, 11
Scott, David (historian) 63
sculpture 10–11, 58
Seaham (County Durham) 10
Seed, Jeremiah (clergyman) 29
Settle, Elkanah (poet, playwright) 21n4
Shaftesbury (Anthony Ashley Cooper), 4th Earl of 6, 17–18, 41, 57
Shaftesbury (Susanna *née* Noel), Countess of 6, 17, 21n10, 51n8
Shakespeare, William 30, 44–5, 49–50, 54, 58; *see also Hamlet, Henry IV Part I, Henry IV Part II, King Lear, The Merry Wives of Windsor, Othello, Richard III, Twelfth Night*
Sharp family 39
Sharp, Francis (musician) 39, 47, 50
Sharp, John (musician) 39
Sharp, Michael (musician) 39
Sherlock, Thomas (churchman) 29, 31
Sherman, Thomas (needleworker: scenery) 43
Short, Thomas (physician) 29
Shropshire, Walter (publisher) 27, 50n2

Shropshire, William (publisher, bookseller) 27, 36, 44, 50n2
Skinner, Mr. 43
Skynner, John 11–12
Smith, Christopher (Handel's amanuensis) 36–7
Smith, James Edward (botanist) 54
Smith, Margaret 1, 2, 41, 44
Smith, Robert (mathematician) 29, 30
Smith, Thomas (painter) 9
Smollett, Tobias (novelist) 44
Southerne, Thomas (dramatist) 44, 45
Spalding (Lincs.) 56–7
Spanish Fryar, The, or The Double Discovery (Dryden) 45
Stamford (Lincs.) 27, 33, 54
Stanhope, Philip *see* Chesterfield
Stanyan, Temple (politician) 29
Steele, Richard (playwright, writer) 30, 45
Stowe (Bucks.) 8–9
Straight & Skillern (publishers) 36
Subscriptions 12–14, 17, 61–4

Tartini, Giuseppe (violinist, composer) 35
Tasso, Torquato (poet) 30
Temple of Apollo, Society of the 34–6
Temple, Richard *see* Cobham, Viscount
Theatre: costumes 49–50; curtains 44; garden theatre 41–2; scenery 41–4, 45–6; soundboard 42; stages 41–4
Theobald, Lewis (editor, playwright) 46, 49
Thomson, James (poet, playwright) 30, 35, 44, 63
Trip to the Jubilee, A, see Constant Couple, The
Twelfth Night (Shakespeare) 49, 58

Uppingham 15

Vasari, Giorgio (painter, architect) 30
Vauxhall Gardens 40, 41
Velde, Willem van der (painter) 10

Venetian Ballads (Hasse) 37
Venice Preserv'd (Otway) 45
Venuti, Niccolò Marcello (artist) 29
Vernon, Mr and Master (singers) 35
Veronese, Paolo (painter) 10
Virgil (Publius Virgilius Maronis) 30
Voice of Melody 34

Wages 21, 25n68, 42, 50n1, 53n36
Walking Statue, The, or The Devil in the Wine-Cellar (Hill) 44
Walmsly, Alice (dealer in stringed instruments) 33, 38
Walsh, John (publisher) 17, 36, 37, 63
Walton, Izaak (writer) 29

Wamsley, Peter (maker of stringed instruments) 33
Wedding of Weddings, The, or Limberhambus Noos'd 3n6
Wellingore (Lincs.) 5
Westminster 5
Weston, William (preacher) 64
Whitmill, Benjamin (gardener) 29
Whitwell (Rutland) 10
Wilson, William 50
Wise, Samuel (composer) 55
Withers, Lieutenant General 9
Wombourne 57
Woodward, Henry (actor) 35
Wright, George (music master) 34, 38

Yardley, Edward (archdeacon of Cardigan) 29

For Product Safety Concerns and Information please contact our EU representative GPSR@taylorandfrancis.com
Taylor & Francis Verlag GmbH, Kaufingerstraße 24, 80331 München, Germany

www.ingramcontent.com/pod-product-compliance
Lightning Source LLC
Chambersburg PA
CBHW051752230426
43670CB00012B/2257